BIG-NOTE PIANO

2ND EDITION

Old Time ROCK 'N' ROLL

ISBN 0-7935-4434-3

HAL•LEONARD®
CORPORATION
7777 W. BLUEMOUND RD. P.O. BOX 13819 MILWAUKEE, WI 53213

Visit Hal Leonard Online at
www.halleonard.com

BE-BOP-A-LULA

Words and Music by TEX DAVIS
and GENE VINCENT

Medium slow Rock

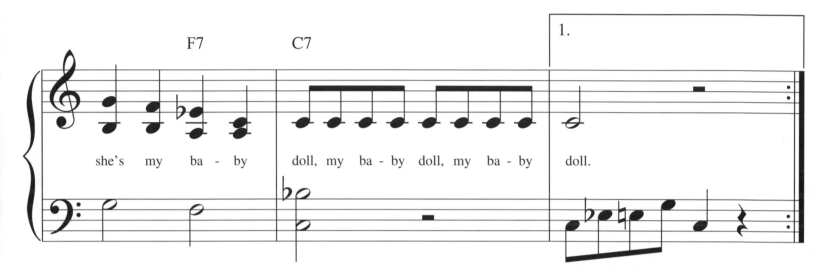

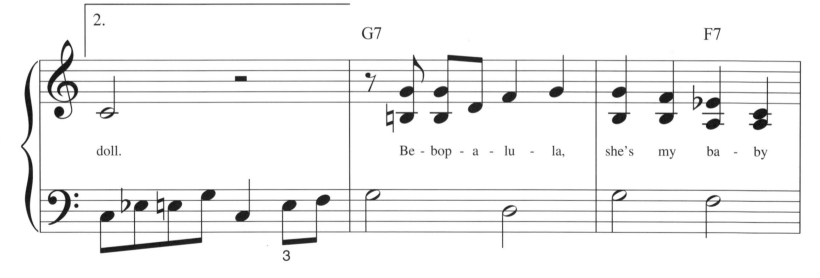

Blue Suede Shoes

Words and Music by
CARL LEE PERKINS

Bright tempo (not too fast)

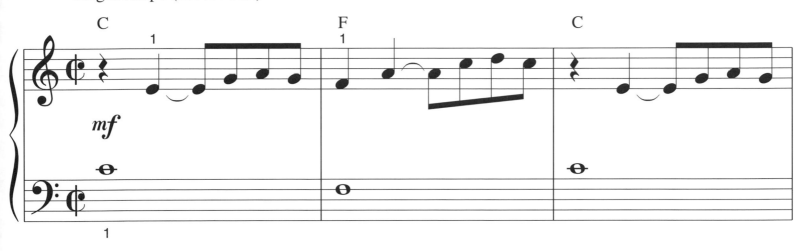

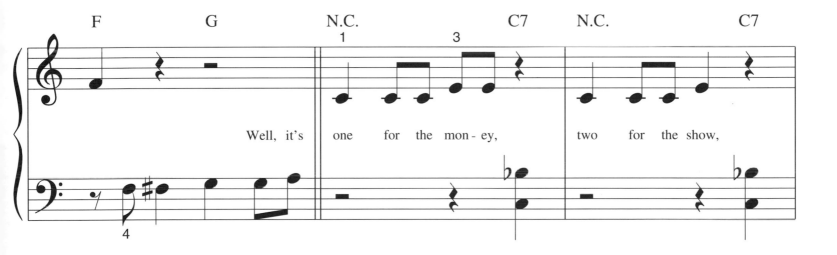

Well, it's one for the mon-ey, two for the show,

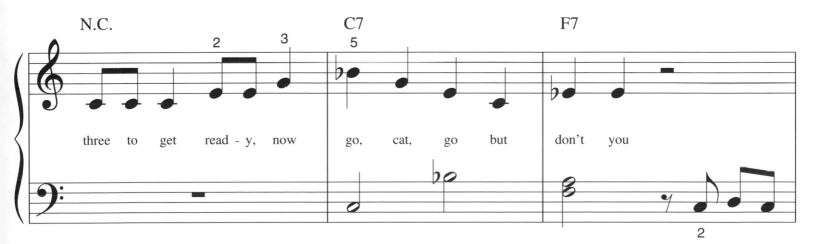

three to get read-y, now go, cat, go but don't you

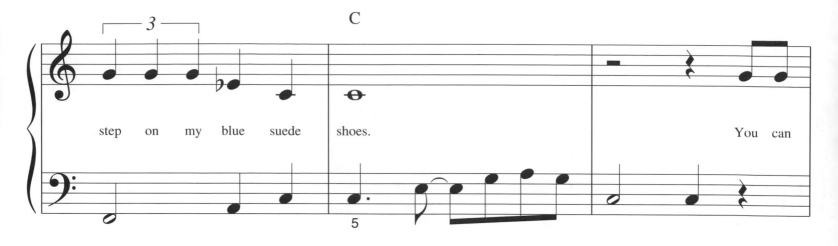

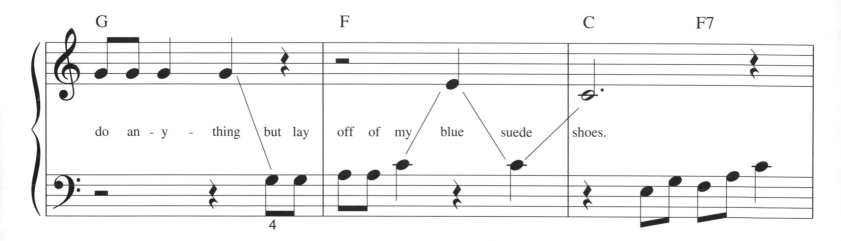

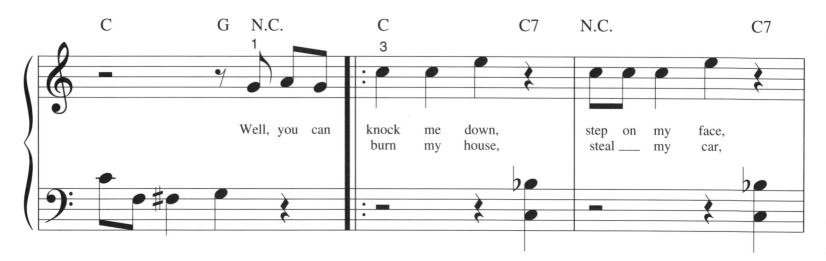

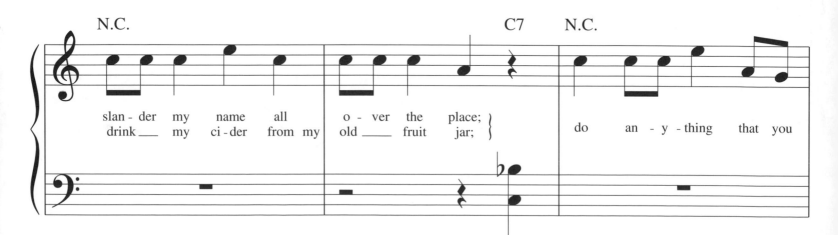

want to do, but uh - uh, hon - ey, lay off of my shoes.

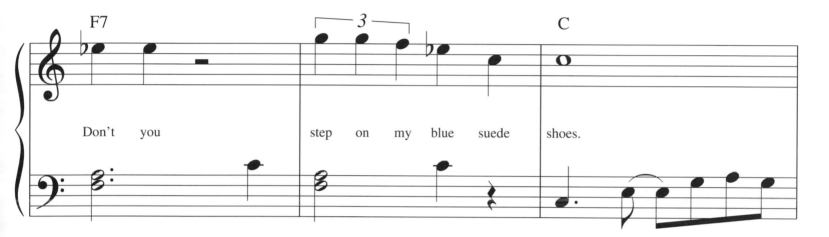

Don't you step on my blue suede shoes.

You can do an - y - thing but lay off of my blue suede

shoes. Well, you can shoes.

DON'T BE CRUEL
(To a Heart That's True)

Words and Music by OTIS BLACKWELL
and ELVIS PRESLEY

Moderately bright, with a beat

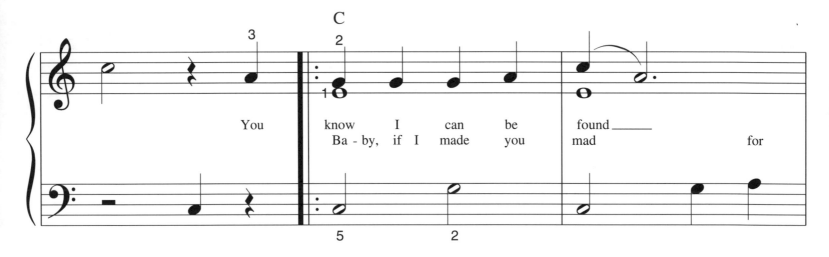

You
Ba - by, if I made you

know I can be
found

mad for

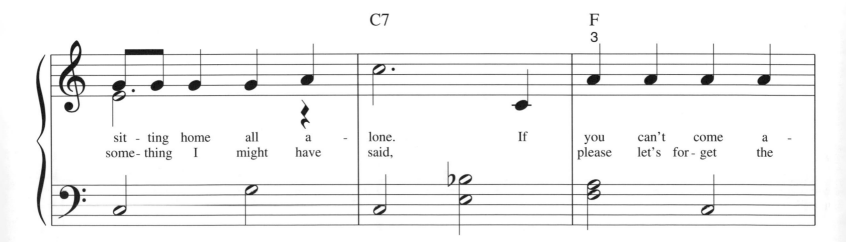

sit - ting home all a - lone.
some - thing I might have said,

If
please let's for - get the

you can't come a -

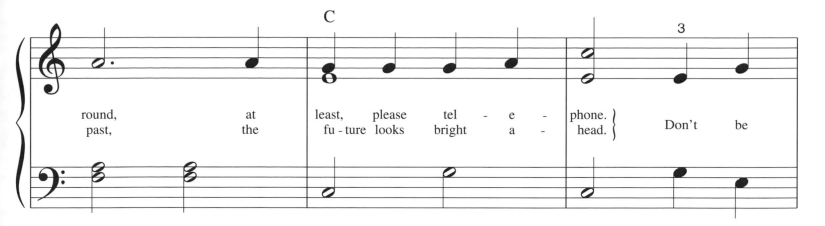

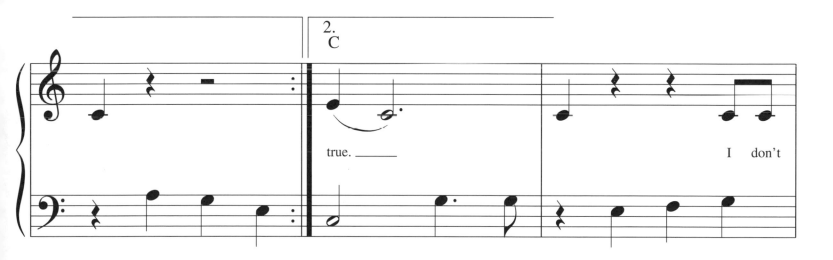

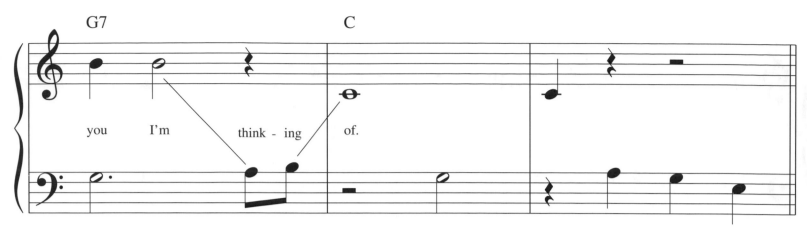

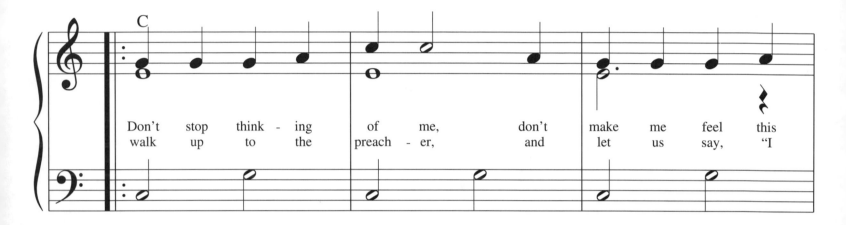

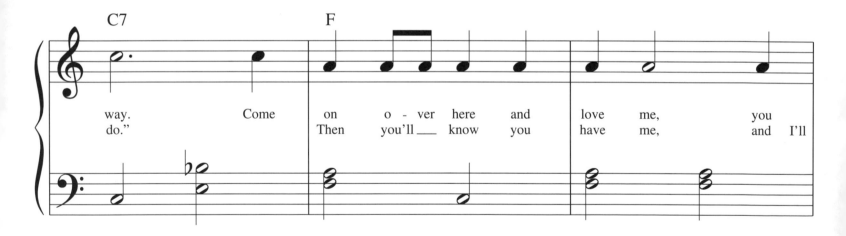

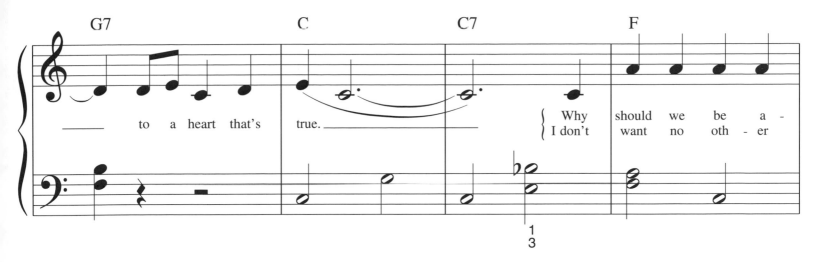

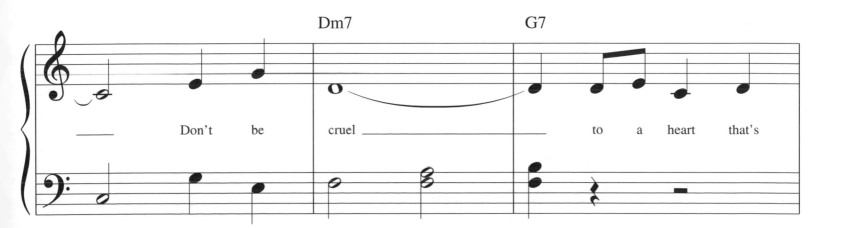

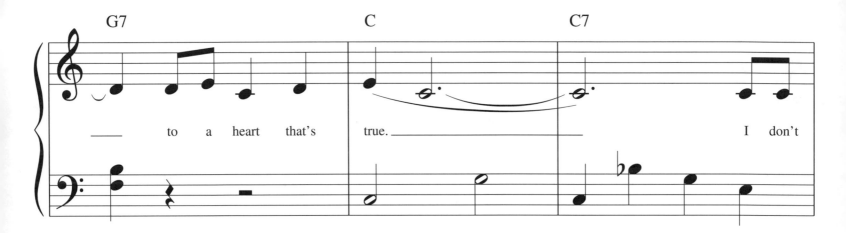

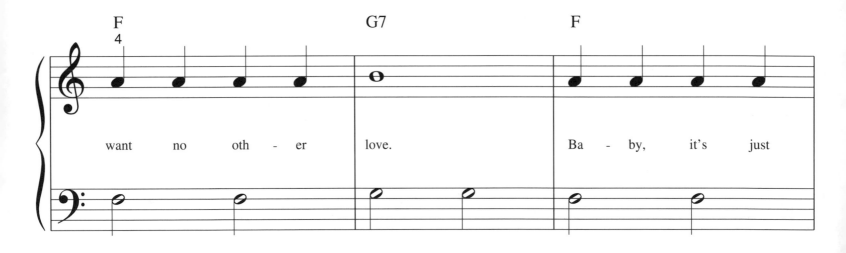

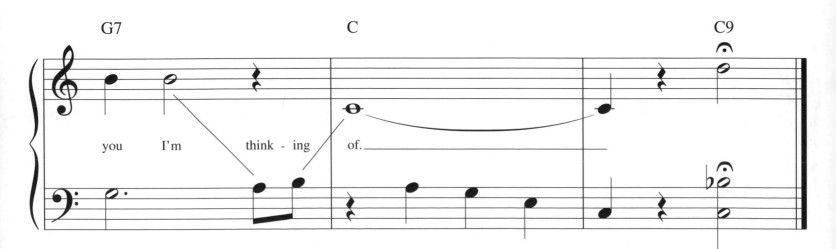

I GET AROUND

Words and Music by BRIAN WILSON
and MIKE LOVE

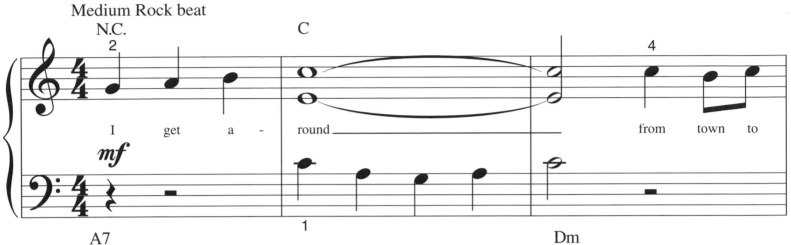

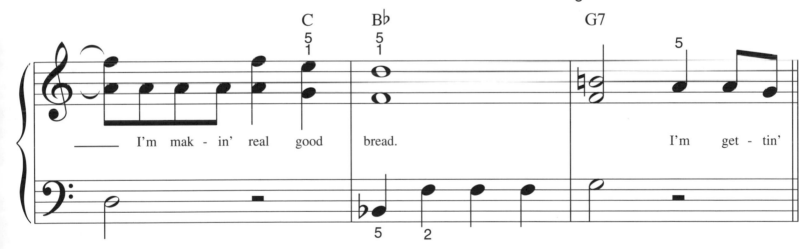

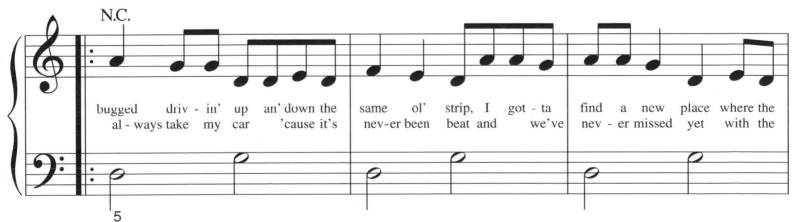

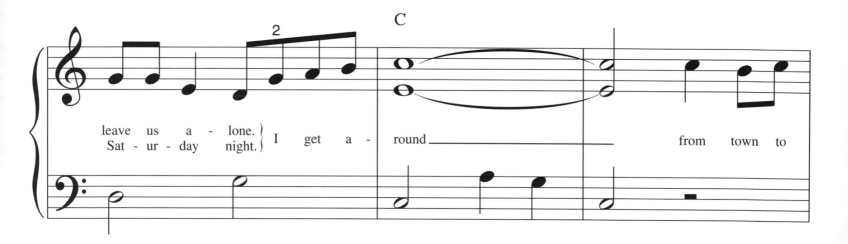

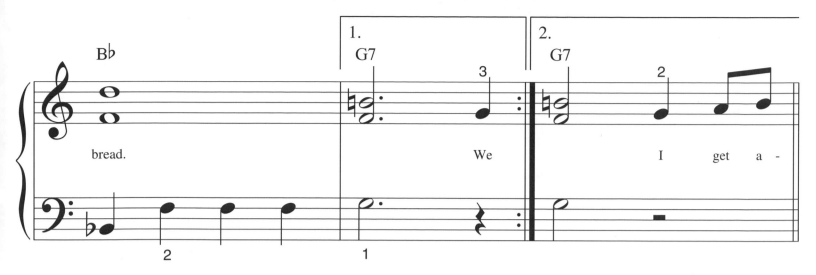

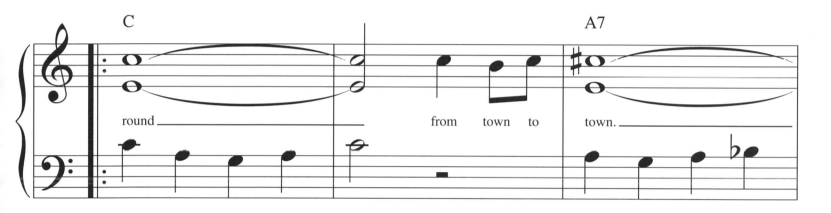

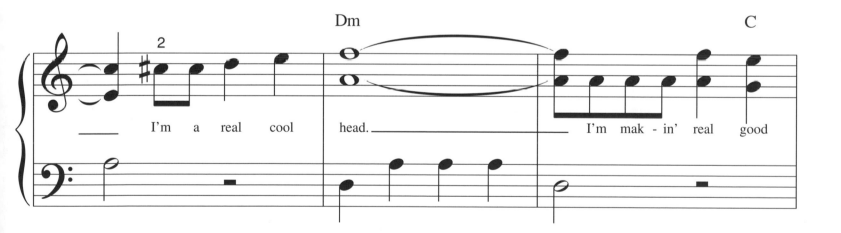

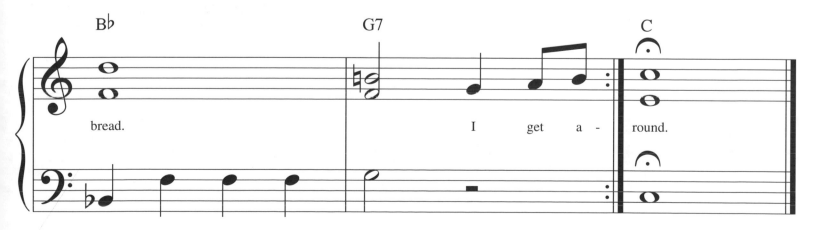

DREAM LOVER

Words and Music by
BOBBY DARIN

Moderately, with a steady beat

Ev-'ry night I hope and pray _____ a dream lov-er will come my way, a girl to hold in my arms _____ and know the mag - ic

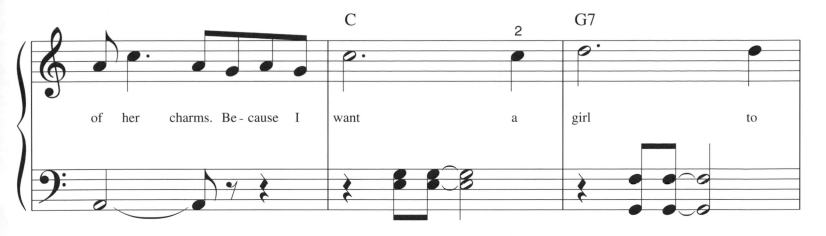

of her charms. Be-cause I want a girl to

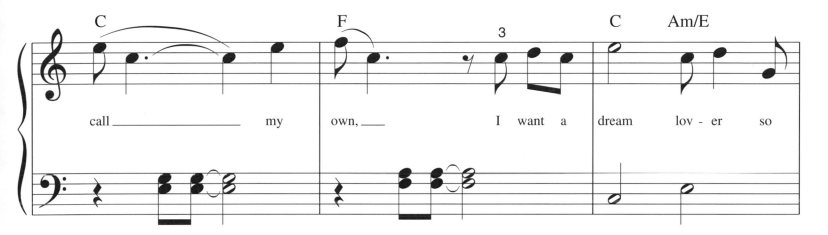

call _____ my own, ____ I want a dream lov-er so

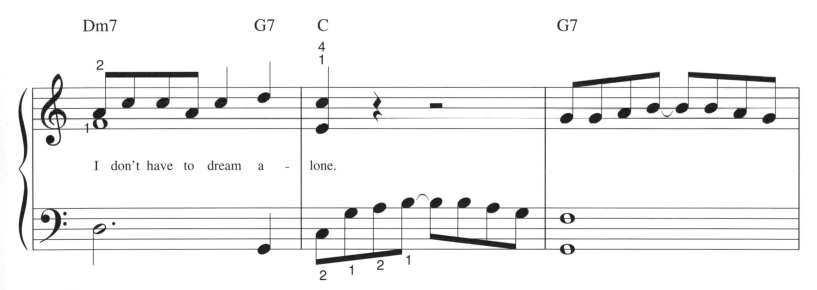

I don't have to dream a - lone.

Dream lov-er, where are you _____ with a love
Dream lov-er, un-til then _____ I'll go to sleep and

To Coda ⊕

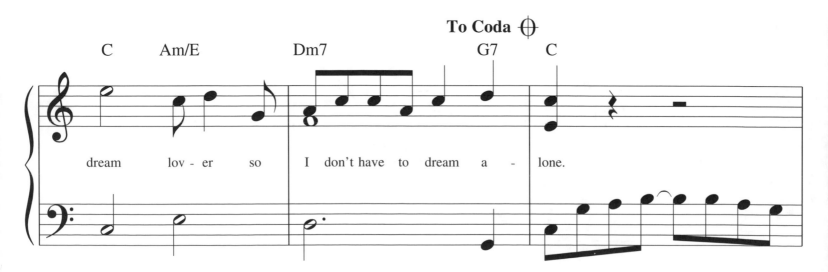

Some day, I don't know how, _____

I hope you'll hear my plea. Some way, I

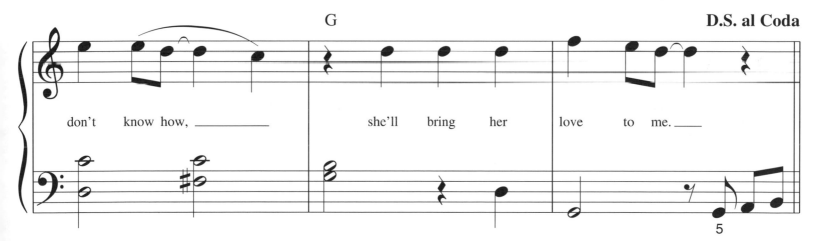

D.S. al Coda

don't know how, _____ she'll bring her love to me. ____

CODA

lone.

GOOD GOLLY MISS MOLLY

Words and Music by ROBERT BLACKWELL
and JOHN MARASCALCO

Moderate Rock 'n' Roll

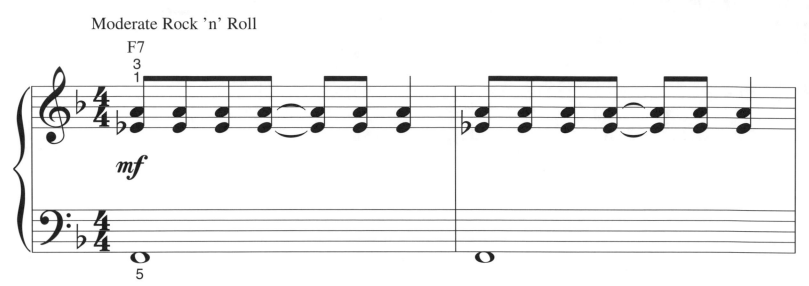

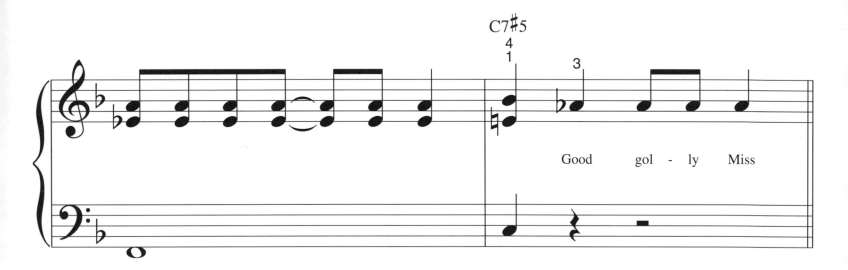

Good gol - ly Miss

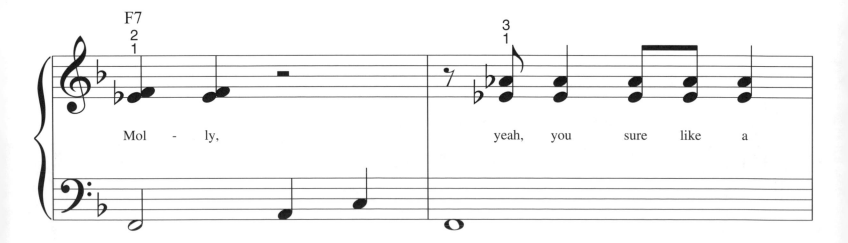

Mol - ly,   yeah, you   sure   like   a

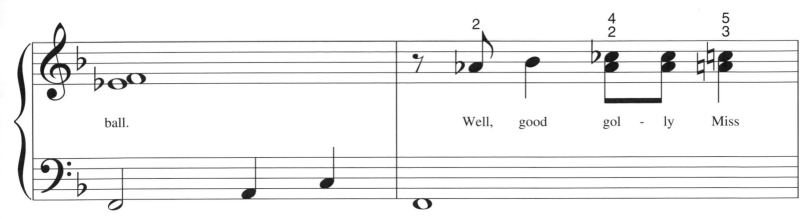

ball.   Well, good gol - ly Miss

Mol - ly,   yeah, you sure like a

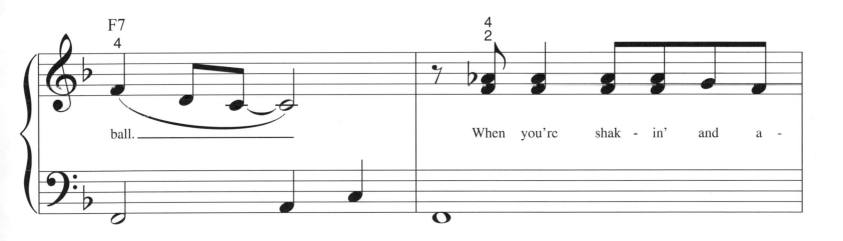

ball. ____   When you're shak - in' and a -

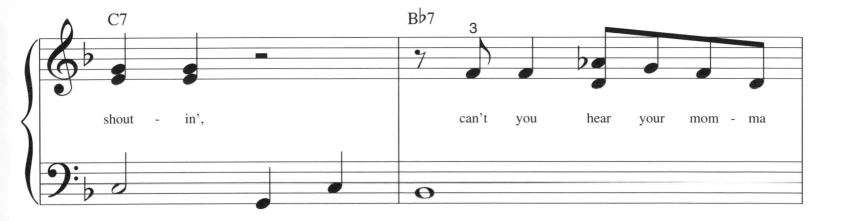

shout - in',   can't you hear your mom - ma

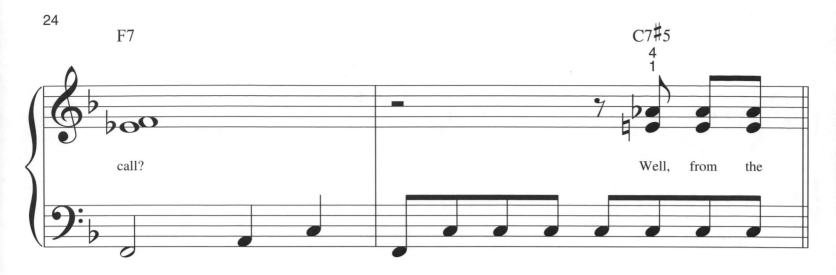

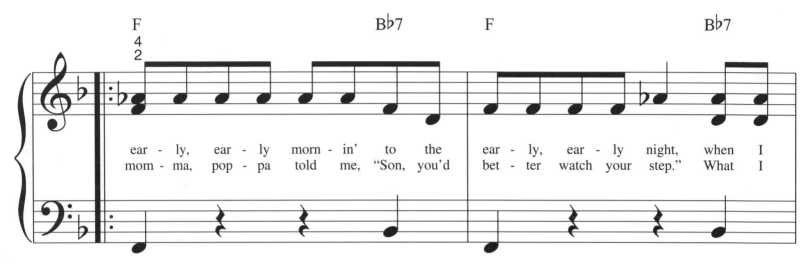

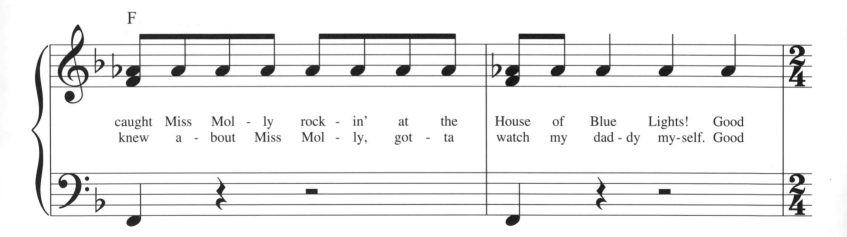

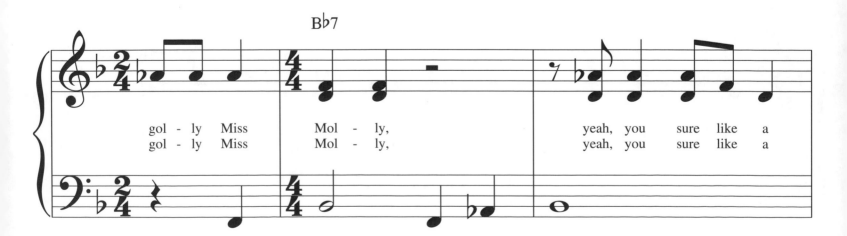

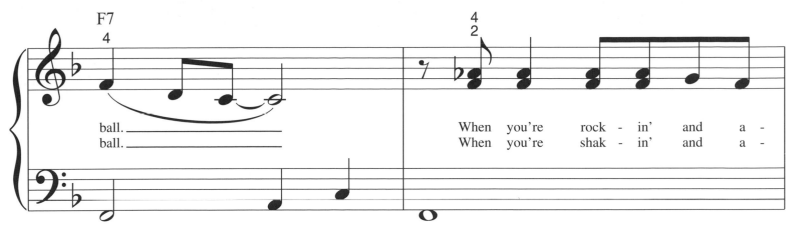

ball. _____
ball. _____

When you're rock - in' and a -
When you're shak - in' and a -

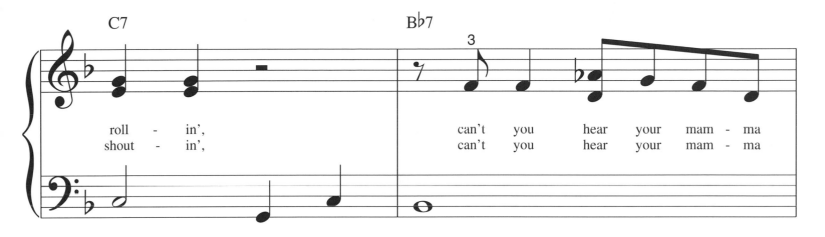

roll - in',
shout - in',

can't you hear your mam - ma
can't you hear your mam - ma

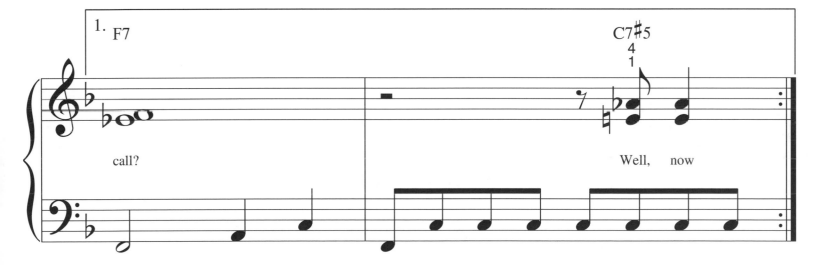

1. call?

Well, now

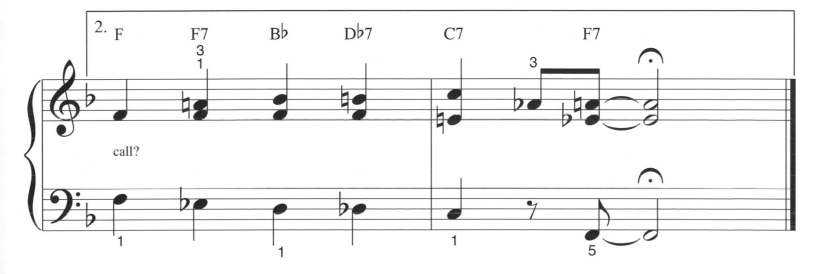

2. call?

GREAT BALLS OF FIRE

Words and Music by OTIS BLACKWELL
and JACK HAMMER

moved me, hon-ey.   I changed my mind,   love's just fine.

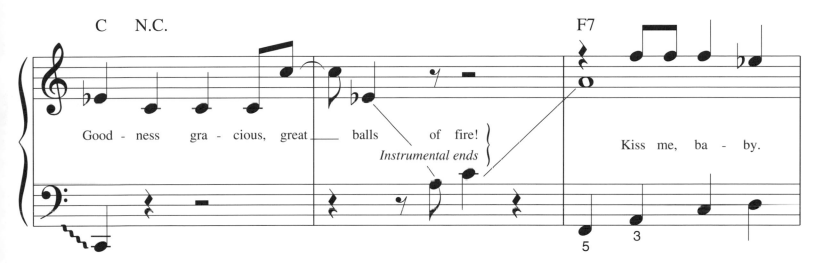

Good - ness gra - cious, great balls of fire!

Instrumental ends

Kiss me, ba - by.

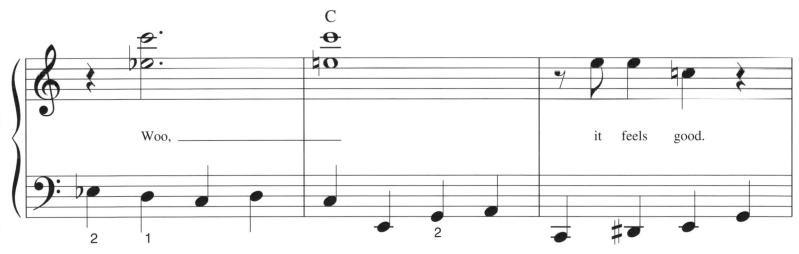

Woo, _____   it feels good.

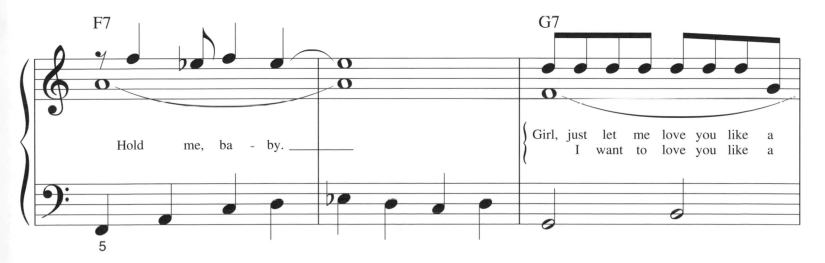

Hold me, ba - by. _____

Girl, just let me love you like a

I want to love you like a

lov - er should.
lov - er should.

You're fine, ___

so kind, ___

I'm gon - na tell the world that you're

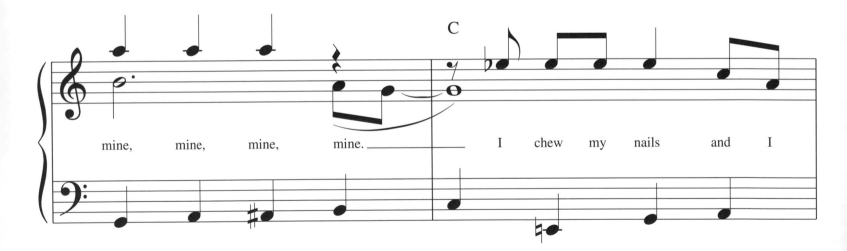

C

mine, mine, mine, mine. ___

I chew my nails and I

F7

twid - dle my thumb.

I'm real nerv - ous but it

sure   is   fun.   Come   on,   ba - by,   you're

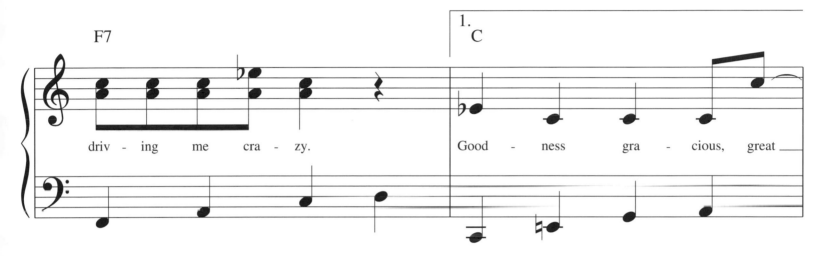

driv - ing   me   cra - zy.   Good - ness   gra - cious,   great

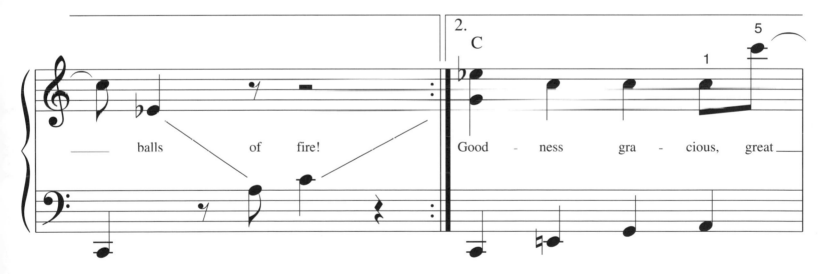

____   balls   of   fire!   Good - ness   gra - cious,   great

____   balls   of   fire!

A GROOVY KIND OF LOVE

Words and Music by TONI WINE
and CAROLE BAYER SAGER

When I'm feel-in' blue, all I have to do is take a look at
want to, you can turn me on to an-y-thing you

you, then I'm not so blue. When you're close to me, I can feel your
want to, an-y-time at all. When I kiss your lips, oo, I start to

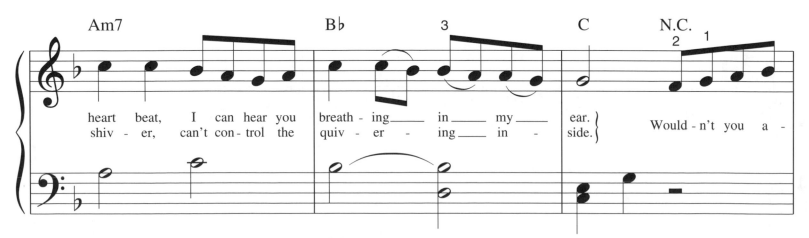

heart beat, I can hear you breath-ing in my ear. Would-n't you a-
shiv-er, can't con-trol the quiv-er-ing in-side.

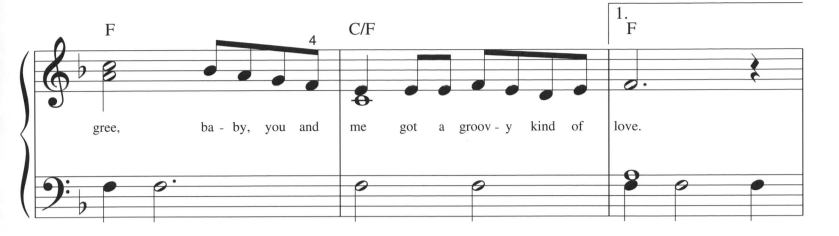

gree,   ba - by, you and   me   got a groov - y kind of   love.

An - y - time you   love.

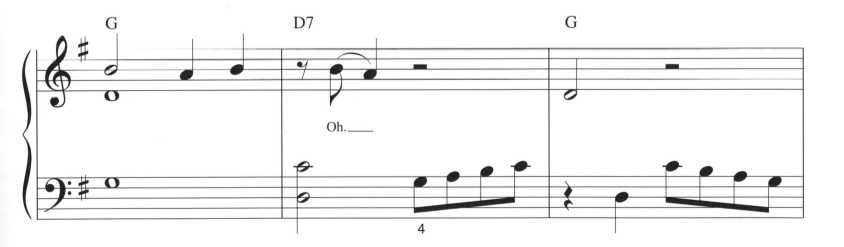

Oh.____

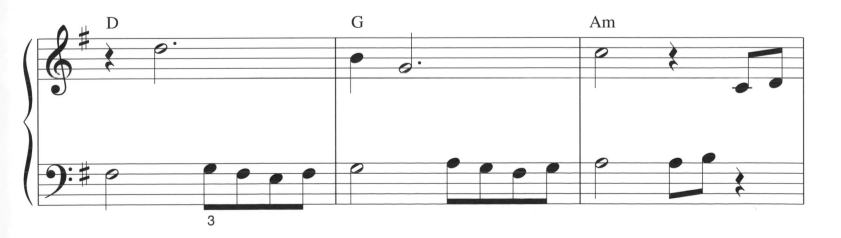

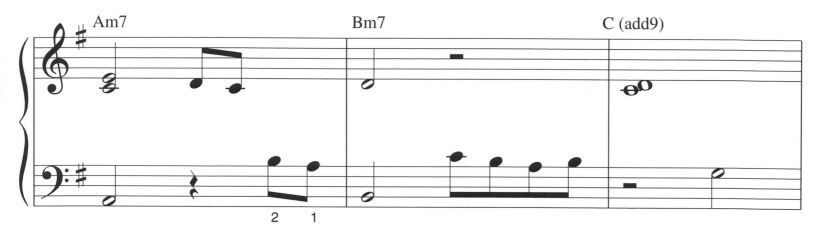

When I'm feel-in' blue, all I got to do is take a look at

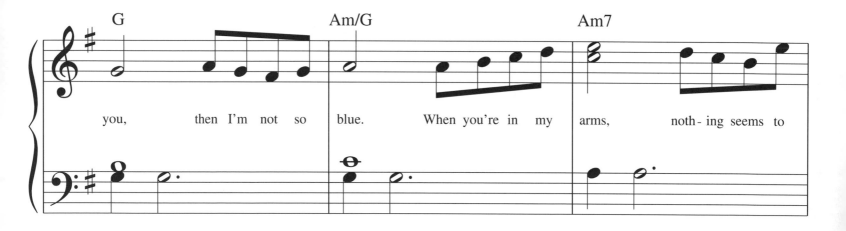

you, then I'm not so blue. When you're in my arms, noth-ing seems to

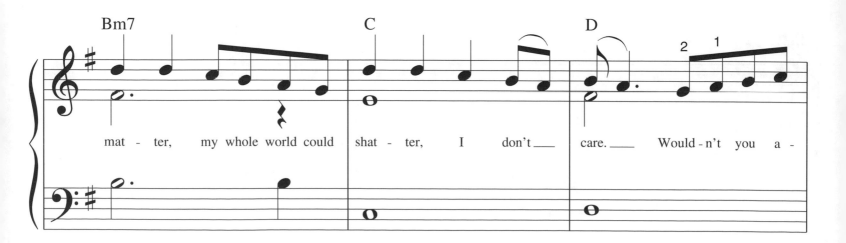

mat-ter, my whole world could shat-ter, I don't___ care.___ Would-n't you a-

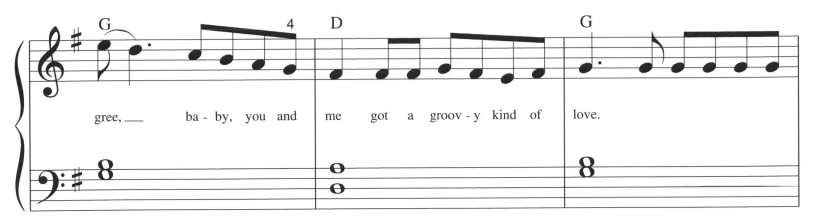

gree, ___ ba - by, you and me got a groov - y kind of love.

We got a groov - y kind of love. We got a groov - y kind of

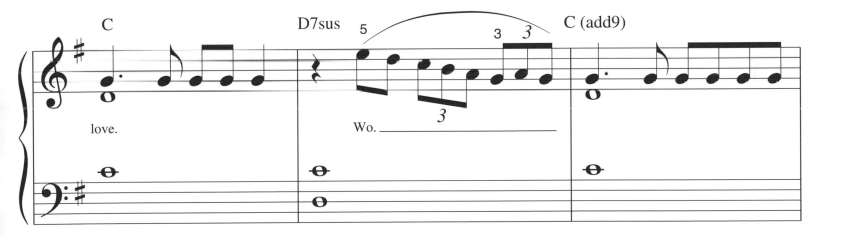

love. Wo. ___

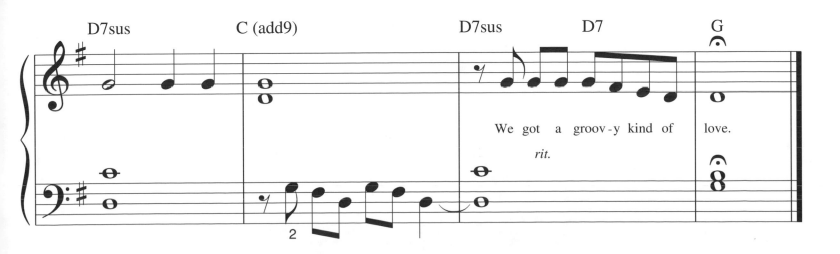

We got a groov - y kind of love.

rit.

LA BAMBA

By RITCHIE VALENS

Moderate Latin beat

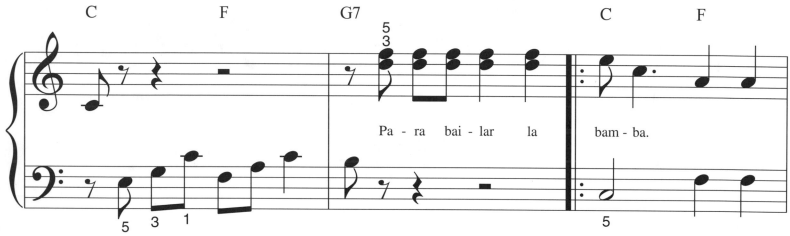

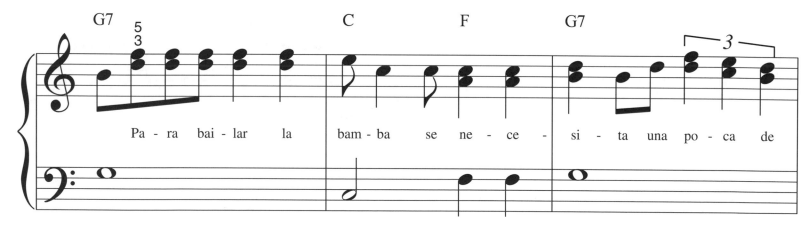

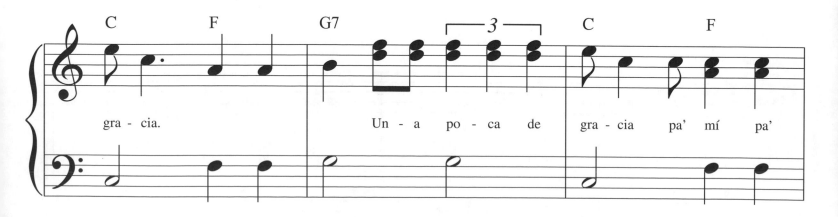

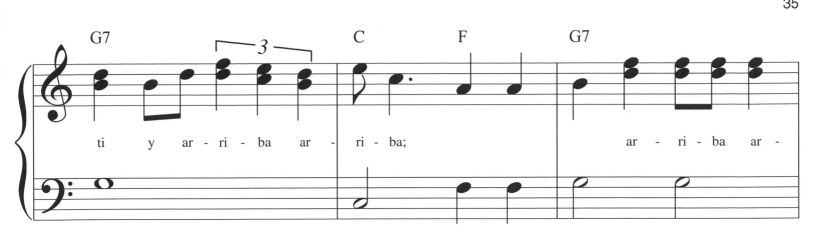

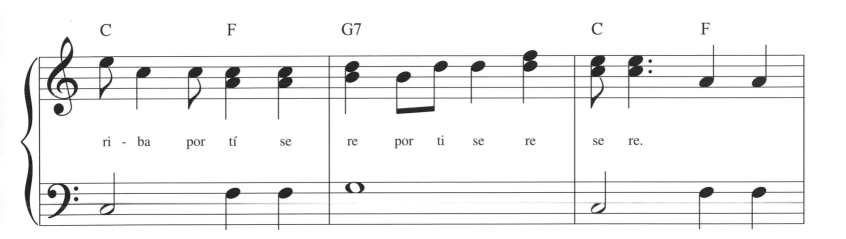

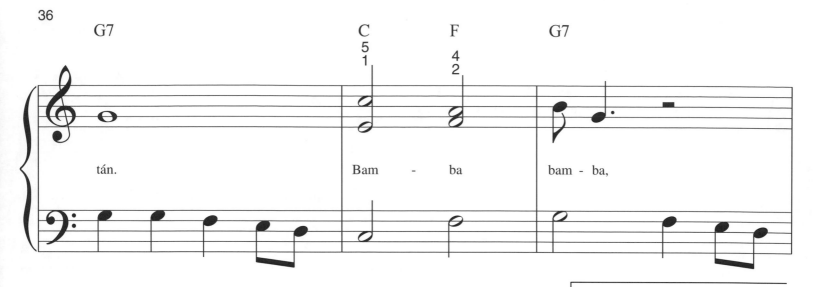

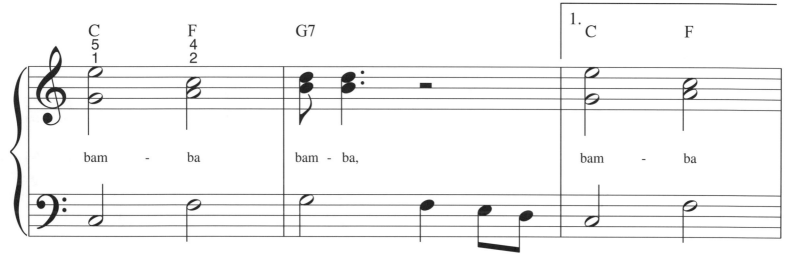

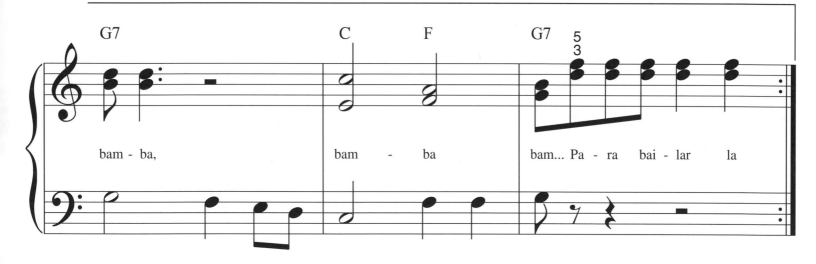

LOUIE, LOUIE

Words and Music by
RICHARD BERRY

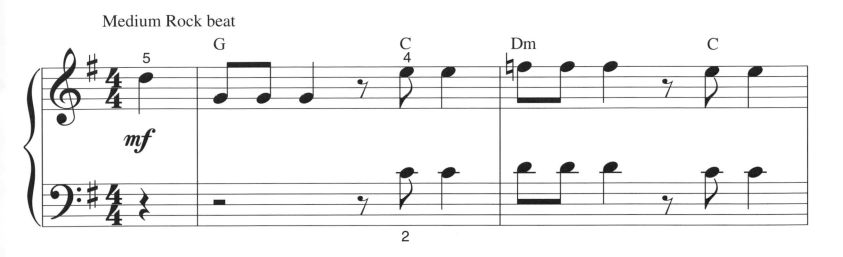

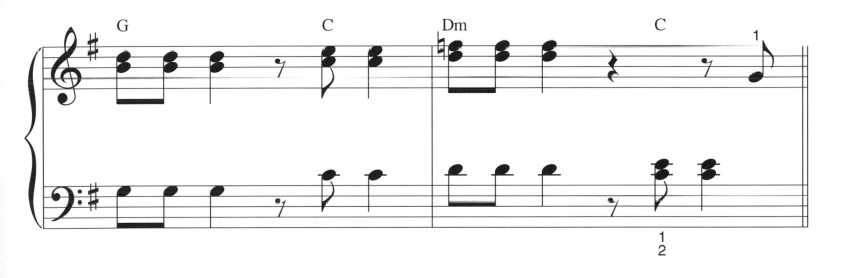

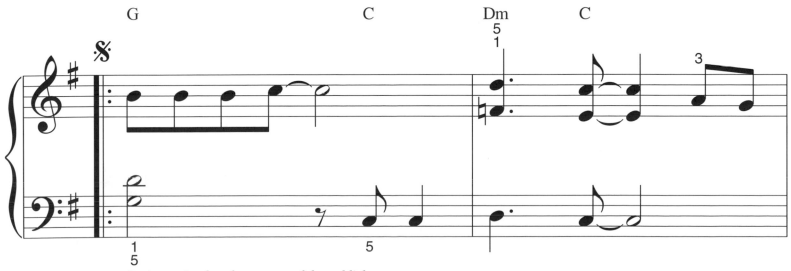

Lyrics omitted at the request of the publisher.

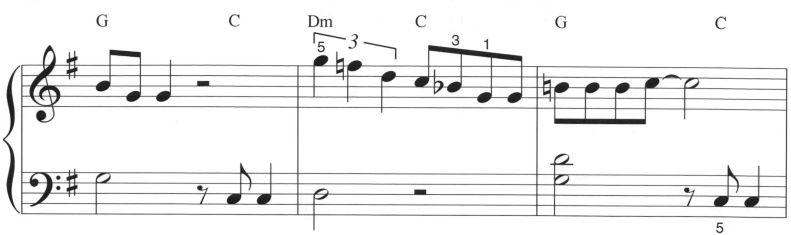

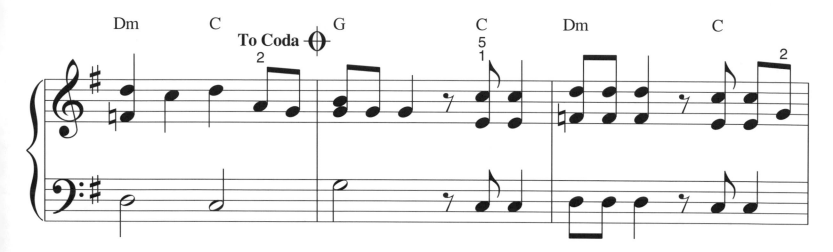

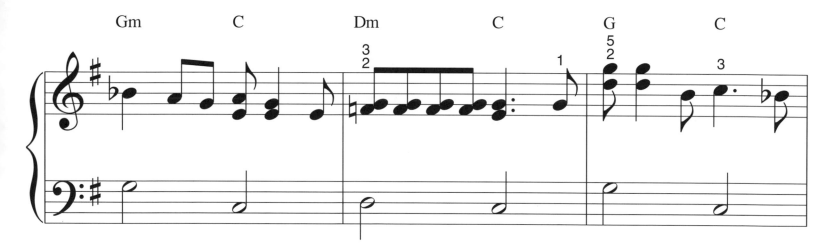

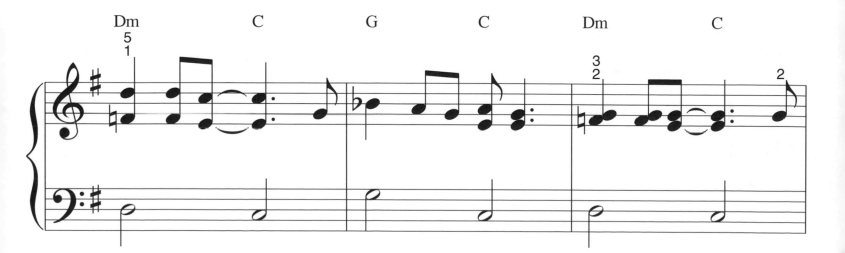

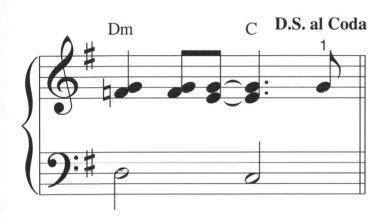

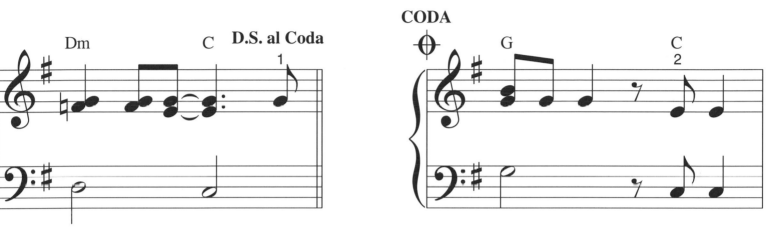

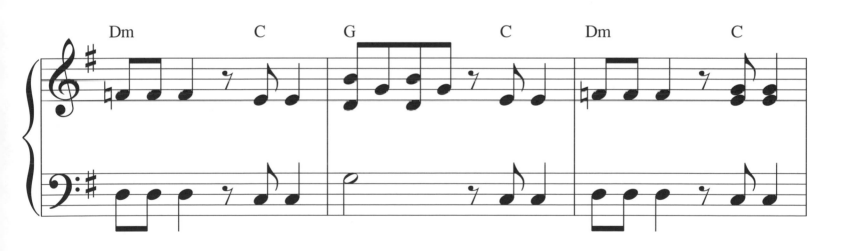

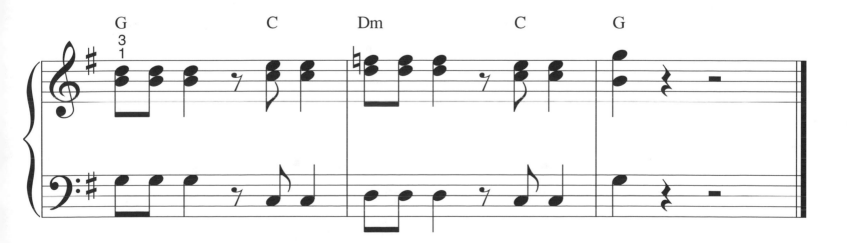

39

THE LOCO-MOTION

Words and Music by GERRY GOFFIN
and CAROLE KING

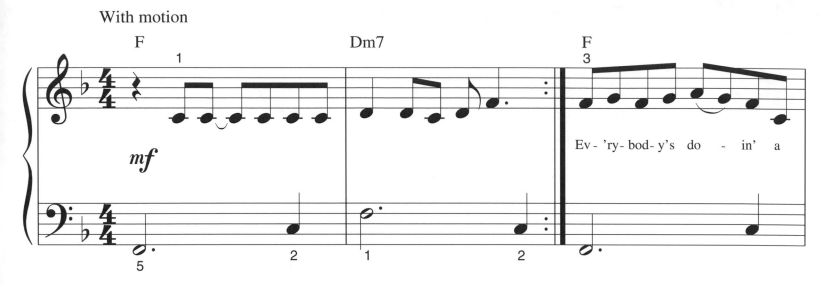

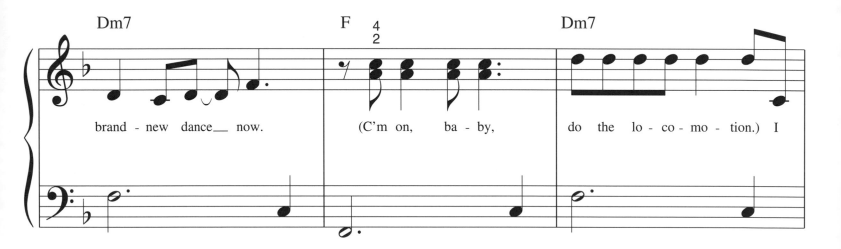

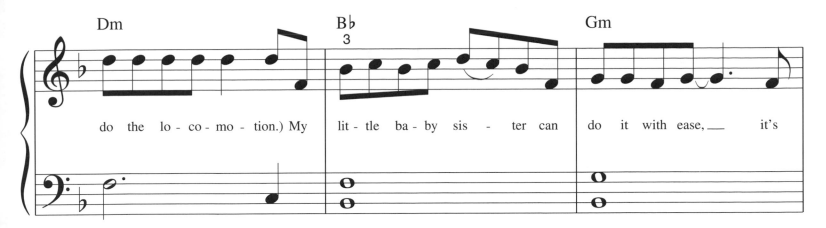

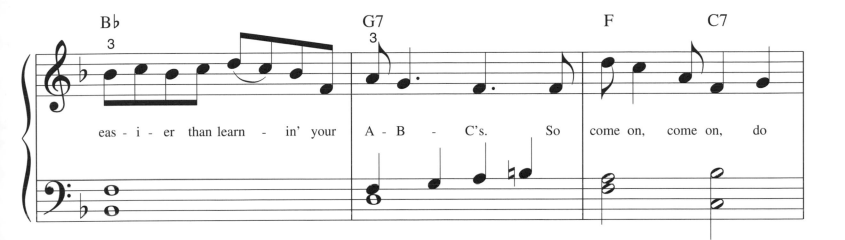

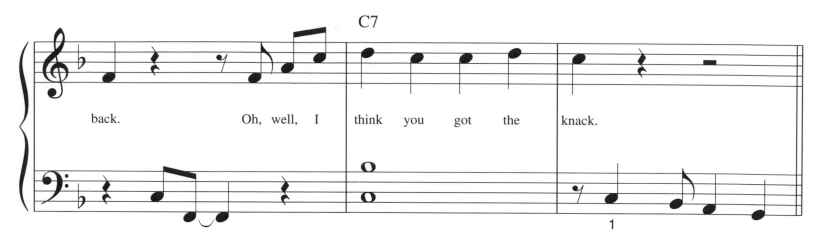

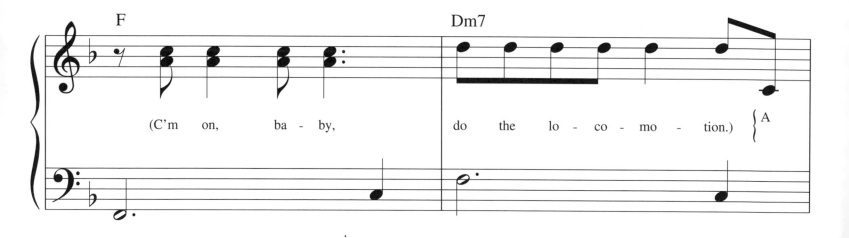

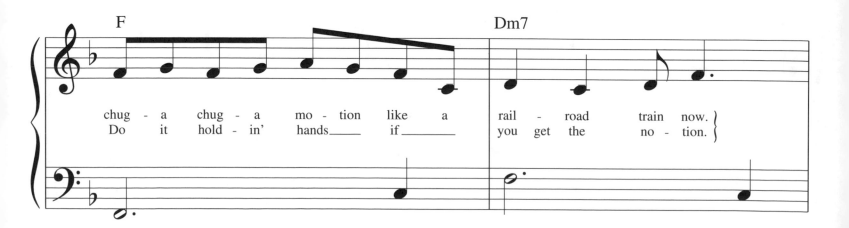

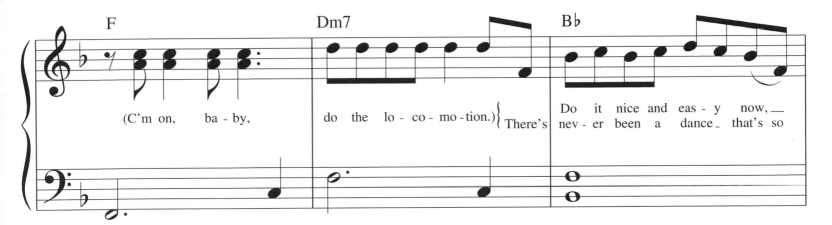

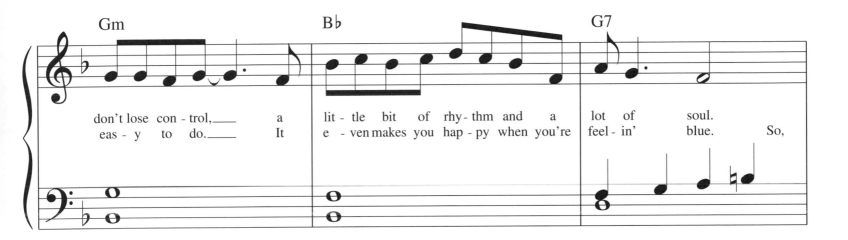

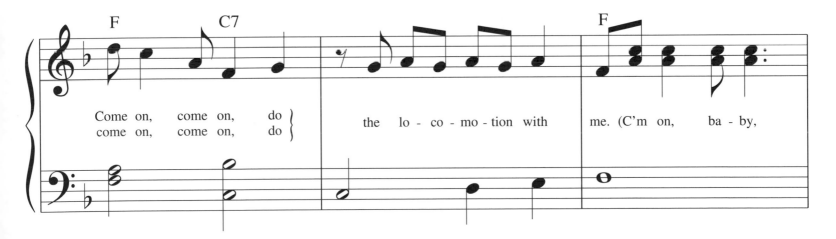

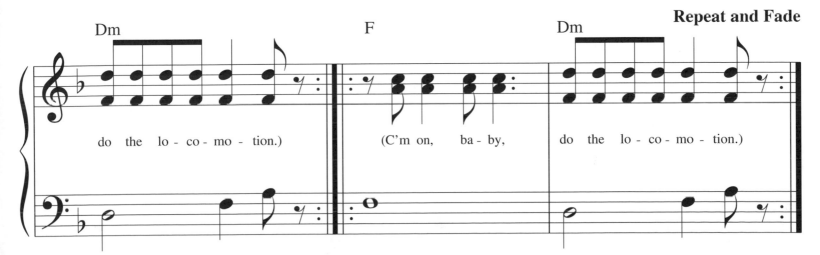

MY BOYFRIEND'S BACK

Words and Music by ROBERT FELDMAN,
GERALD GOLDSTEIN and RICHARD GOTTEHRER

Brightly, with a beat

My boy - friend's back and you're gon - na be in trou - ble.
He's been gone for such a long time. ____

When you see him com - in', bet - ter
Now he's back ____ and ____

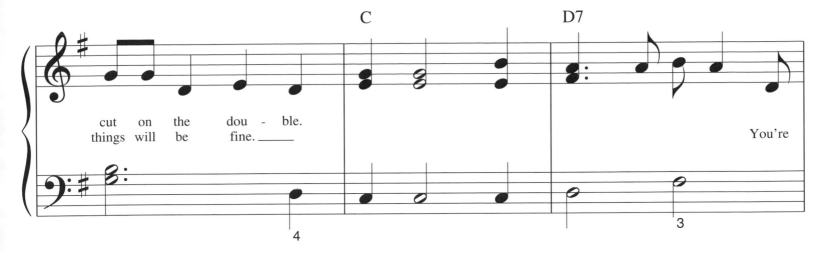

cut on the dou - ble.
things will be fine. _____ You're

You've been spread - in' lies that
gon - na be sor - ry you

I was un - true. _____
ev - er were born. _____

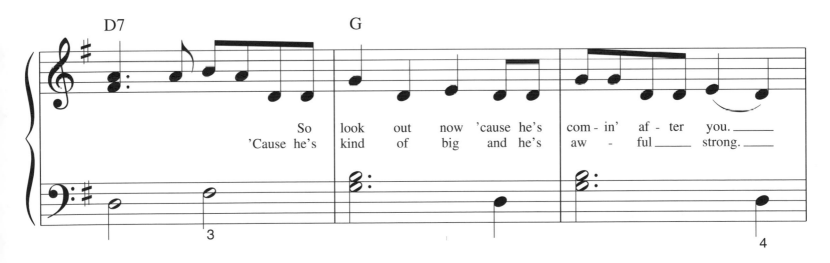

So look out now 'cause he's
'Cause he's kind of big and he's

com - in' af - ter you. _____
aw - ful _____ strong. _____

And he
And he

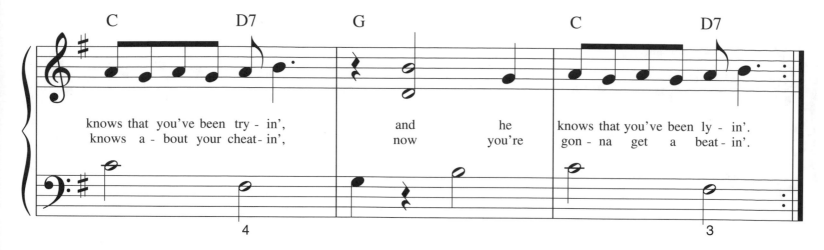

knows that you've been try - in',
knows a - bout your cheat - in',
and he knows that you've been ly - in'.
now you're gon - na get a beat - in'.

What made you think he'd be - lieve all your lies?____

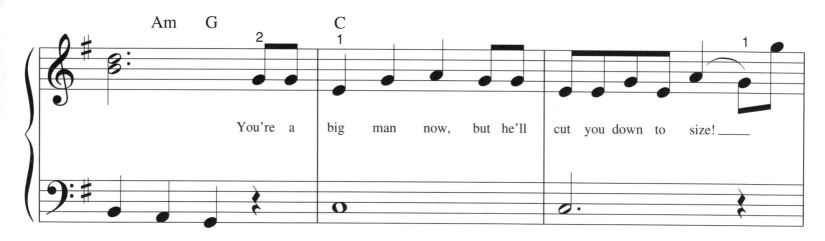

You're a big man now, but he'll cut you down to size!____

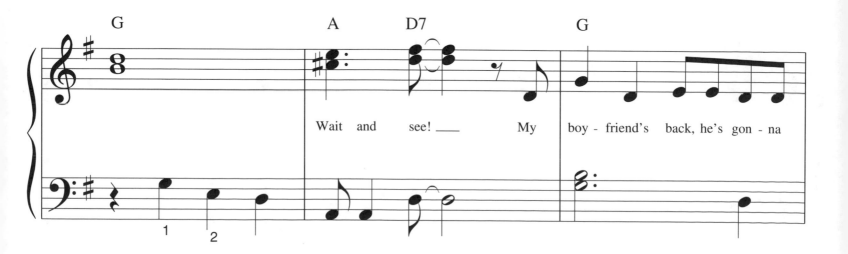

Wait and see! ____ My boy - friend's back, he's gon - na

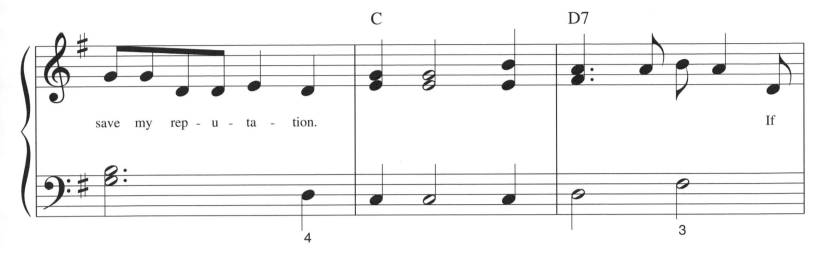

save my rep - u - ta - tion.

If

I were you, I'd take a per - ma - nent va - ca - tion.

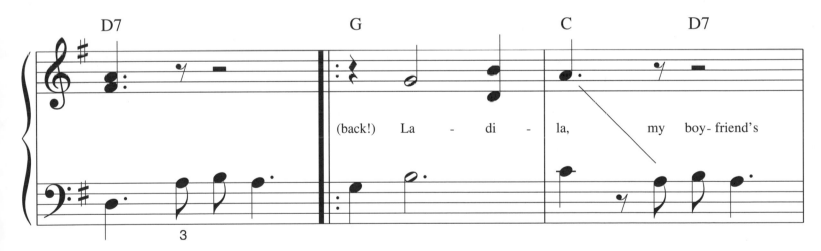

(back!) La - di - la, my boy - friend's

Repeat and Fade

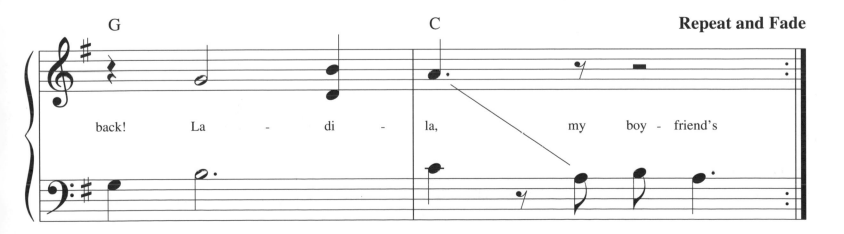

back! La - di - la, my boy - friend's

OH, PRETTY WOMAN

Words and Music by ROY ORBISON
and BILL DEES

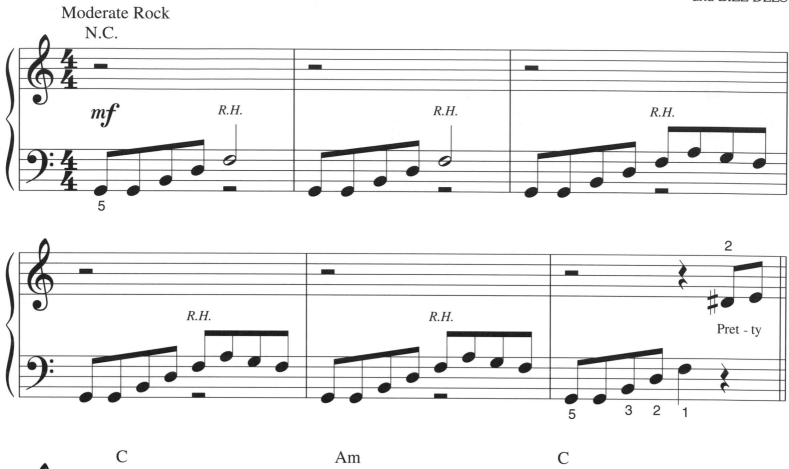

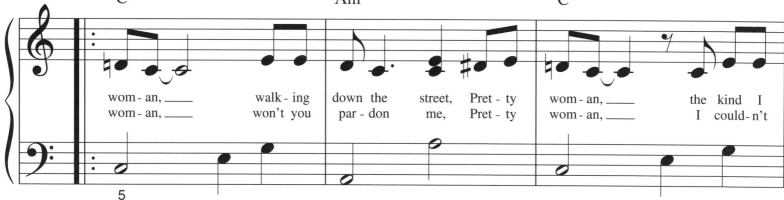

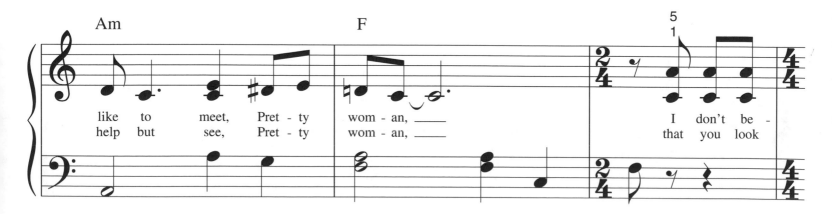

lieve you, _____ you're not the truth.
love-ly _____ as can be.

No one could look as good as
Are you lone - ly just as like

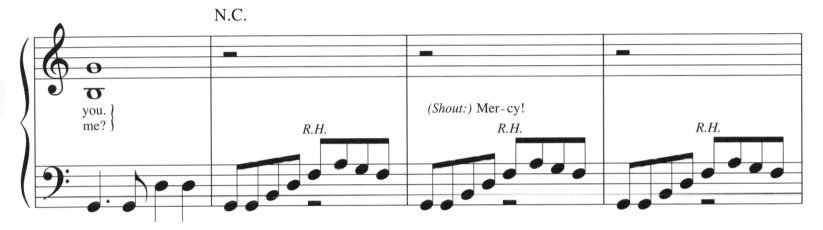

you.
me?

(Shout:) Mer-cy!

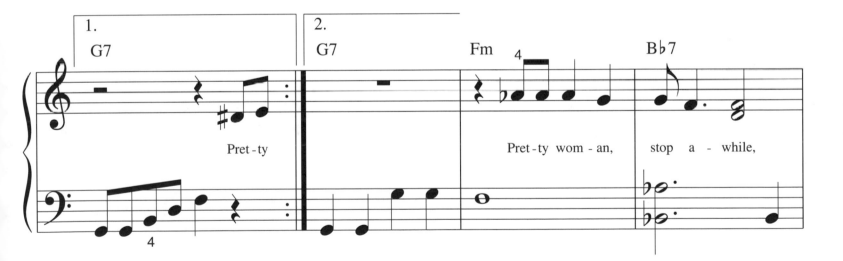

1. G7

2. G7

Fm

B♭7

Pret-ty

Pret-ty wom - an, stop a - while,

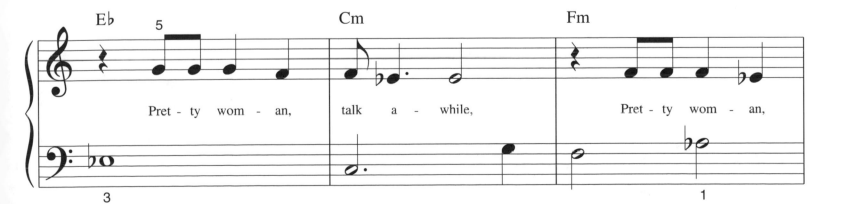

E♭

Cm

Fm

Pret-ty wom - an, talk a - while, Pret-ty wom - an,

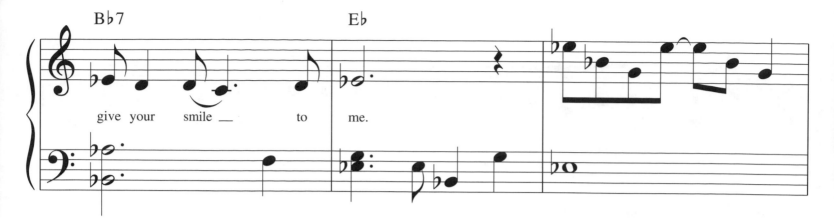

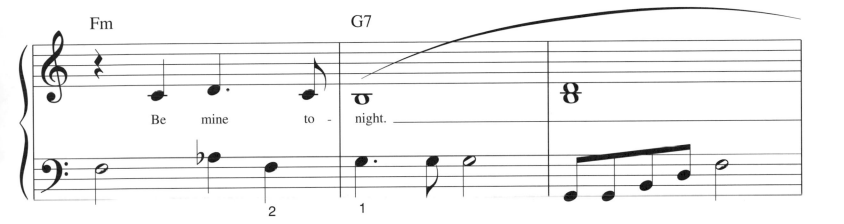

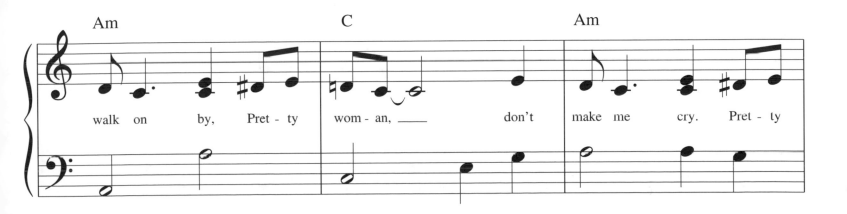

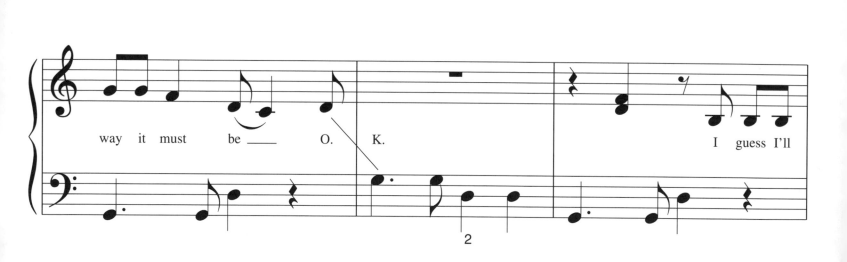

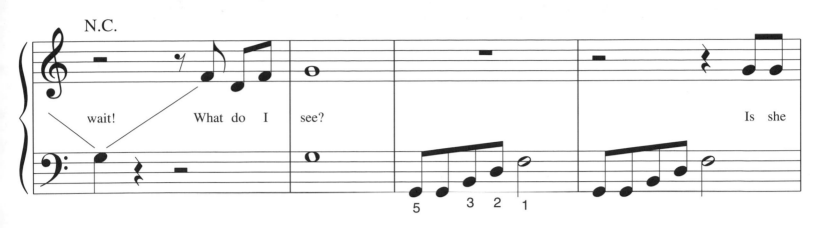

ROCK AROUND THE CLOCK

Words and Music by MAX C. FREEDMAN
and JIMMY DeKNIGHT

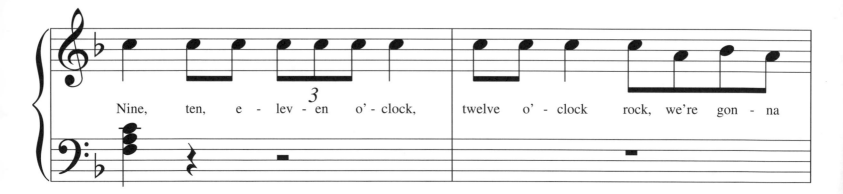

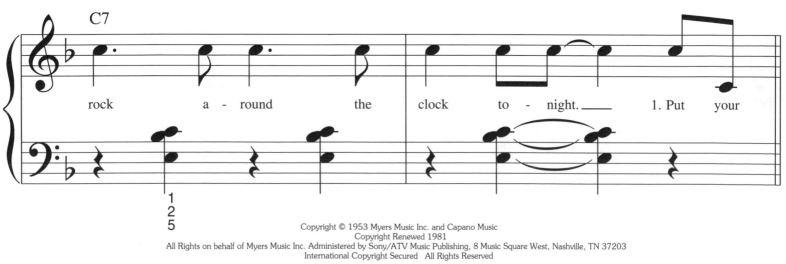

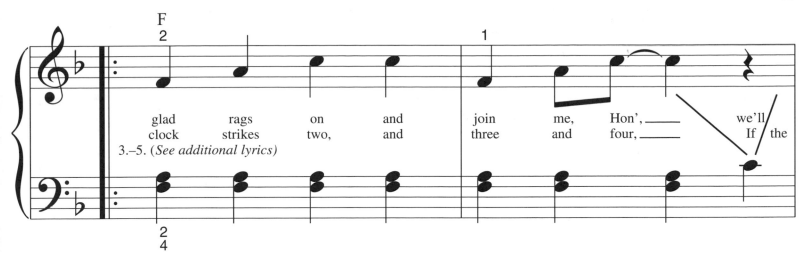

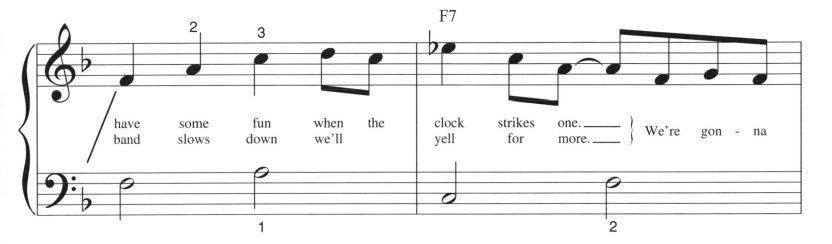

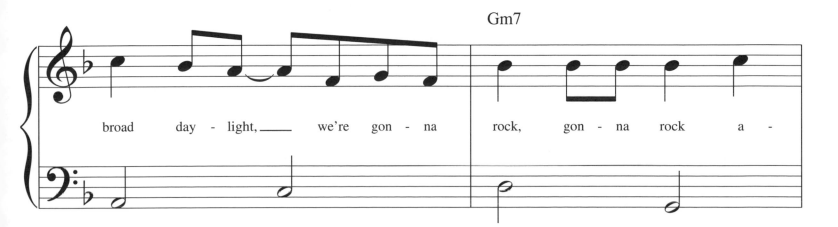

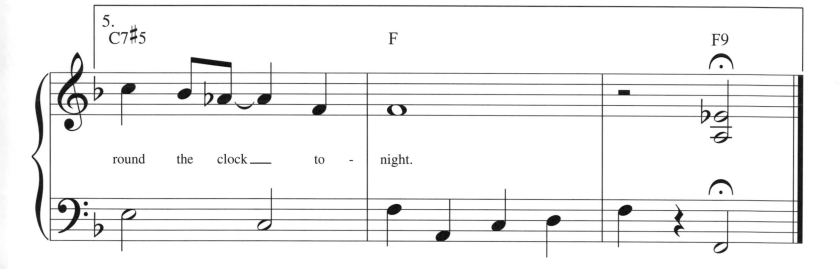

Additional Lyrics

3. When the chimes ring five and six and seven,
   We'll be rockin' up in seventh heav'n.
   We're gonna rock around the clock tonight,
   We're gonna rock, rock, rock 'til broad daylight.
   We're gonna rock, gonna rock around the clock tonight.

4. When it's eight, nine, ten, eleven, too,
   I'll be goin' strong and so will you,
   We're gonna rock around the clock tonight,
   We're gonna rock, rock, rock 'til broad daylight.
   We're gonna rock, gonna rock around the clock tonight.

5. When the clock strikes twelve, we'll cool off, then,
   Start a-rockin' 'round the clock again,
   We're gonna rock around the clock tonight,
   We're gonna rock, rock, rock 'til broad daylight.
   We're gonna rock, gonna rock around the clock tonight.

WILD THING

Words and Music by
CHIP TAYLOR

Moderately, with a beat

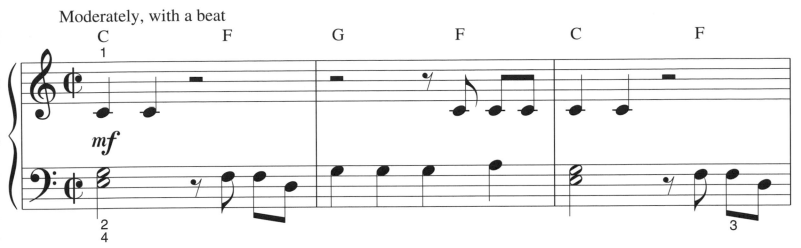

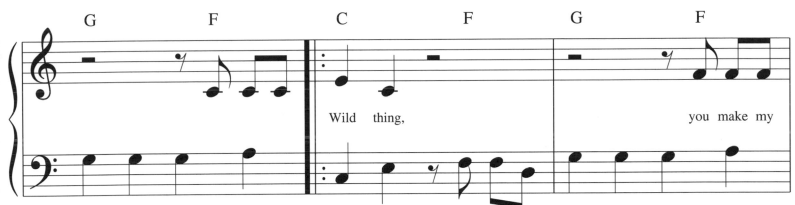

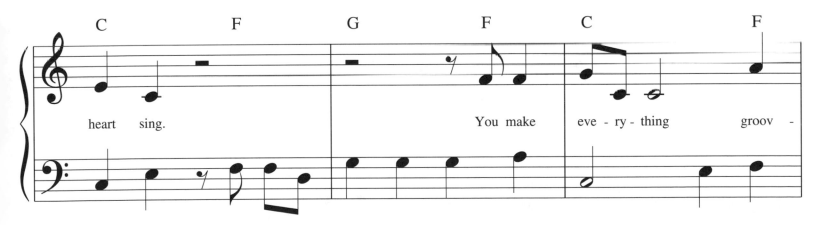

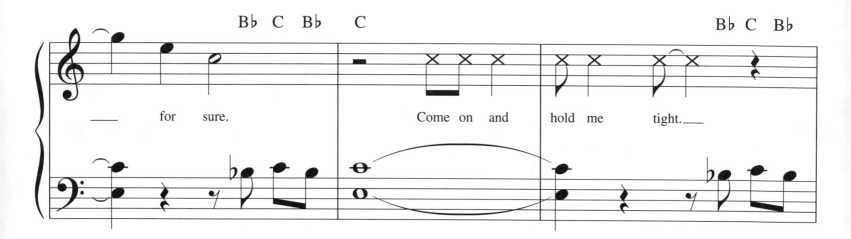

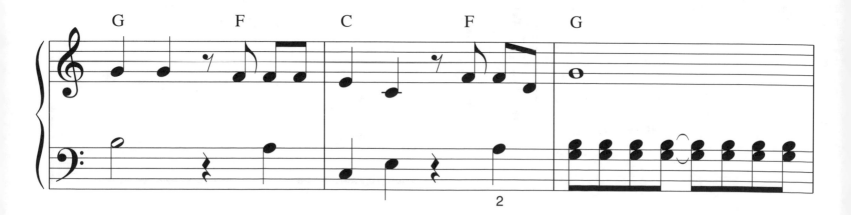

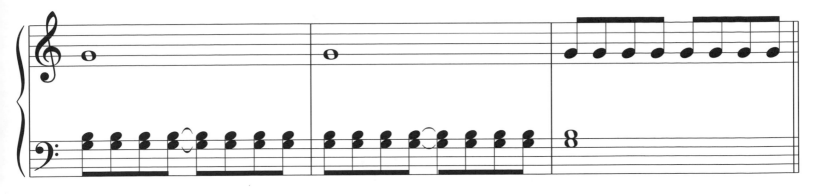

Wild thing, you make my heart sing.

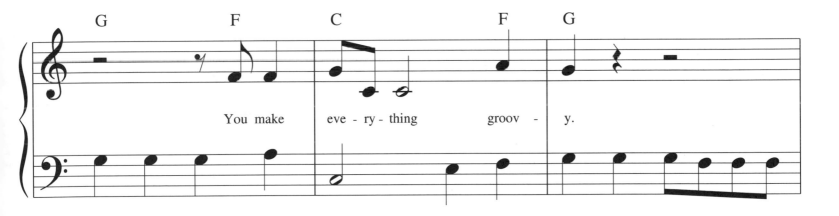

You make eve - ry - thing groov - y.

Repeat and Fade

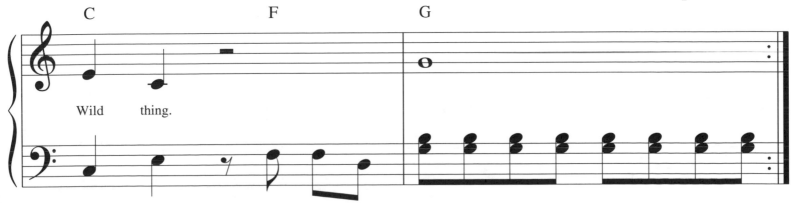

Wild thing.

RUNAWAY

Words and Music by DEL SHANNON
and MAX CROOK

strong.

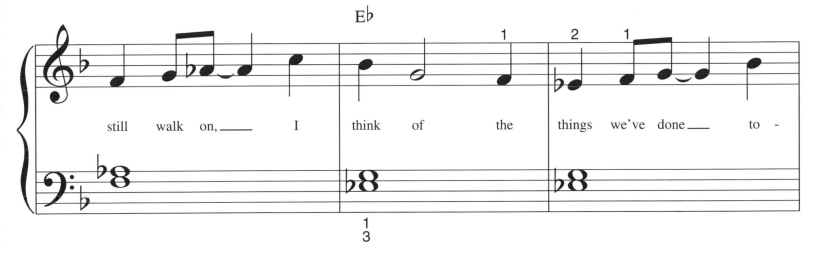

And as I

still walk on,____ I think of the things we've done____ to-

geth - er while our hearts____ were young.

I'm a-walk-in' in the rain.____

Tears are fall - in' and I feel a pain,_____ a - wish - in' you were

here by me_____ to end this mis - er - y._____ And I

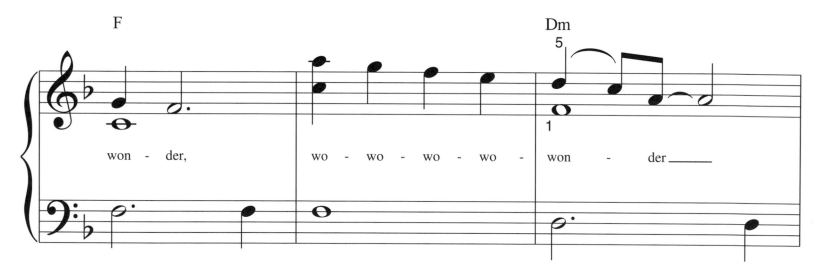

won - der, wo - wo - wo - wo - won - der_____

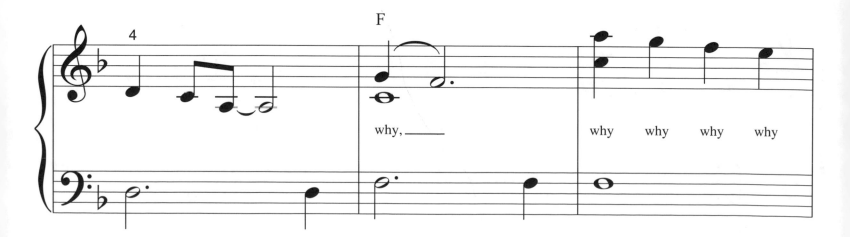

why,_____ why why why why

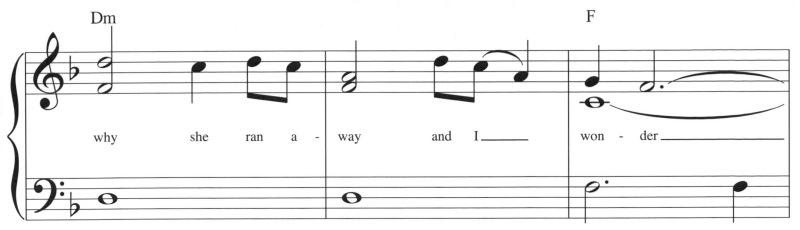

why   she   ran   a - way   and   I____   won - der _____

____   where   she   will   stay, _____   my   lit - tle

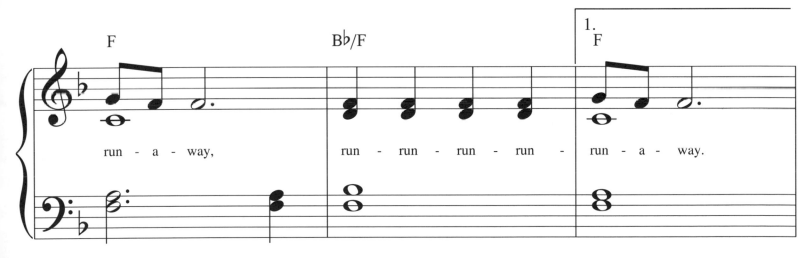

run - a - way,   run - run - run - run -   run - a - way.

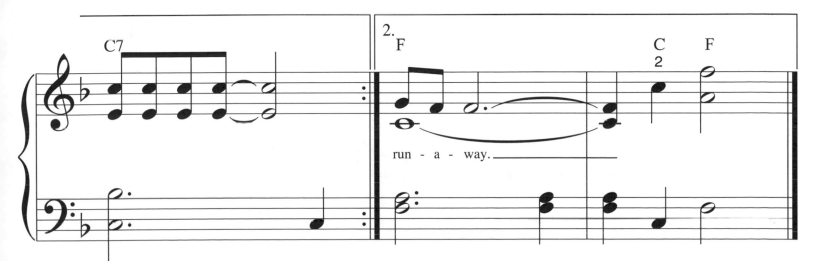

run - a - way. ____

SPLISH SPLASH

Words and Music by BOBBY DARIN
and MURRAY KAUFMAN

Moderately, with a beat

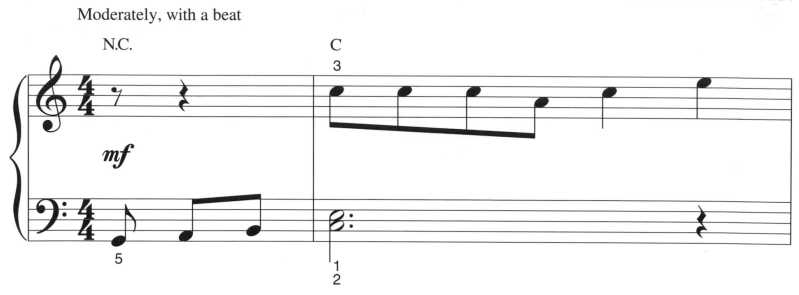

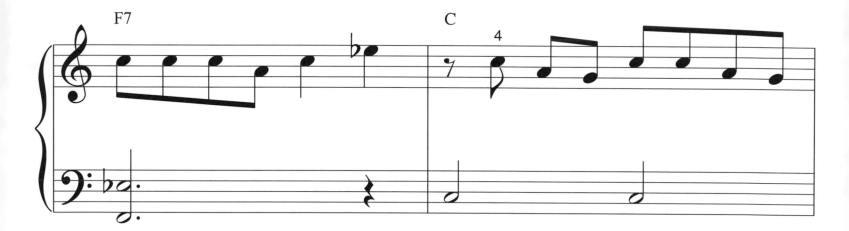

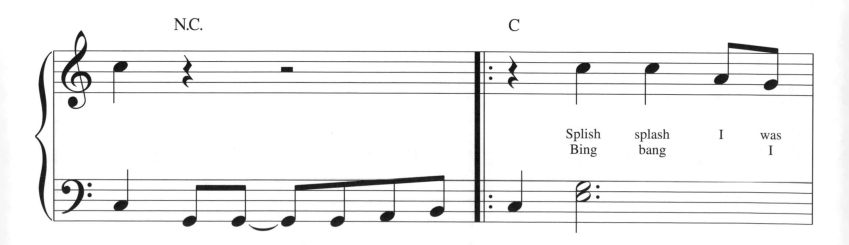

Splish   splash   I   was
Bing   bang   I

tak - in' a bath _____
saw the whole gang _____

'long a - bout a Sat - ur - day
danc - in' on my liv - in' room

night.
rug.

A rub dub, just re
Flip flop, just they were

D7

lax - in' in the tub,
do - in' the _____ bop, all the

think - in' ev - 'ry - thing was all
teens _____ had the danc - in'

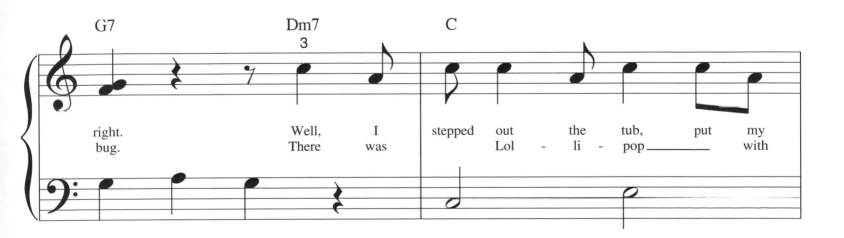

G7   Dm7   C

right.
bug.

Well, I
There was

stepped out the tub, put my
Lol - li - pop _____ with

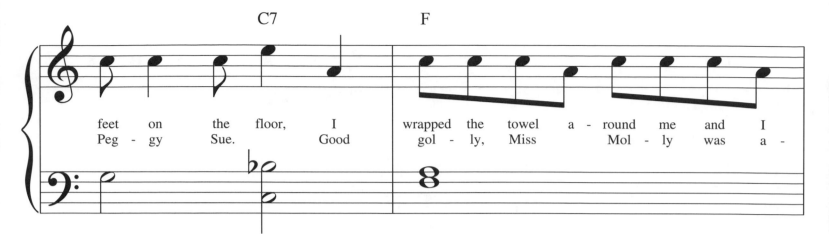

feet on the floor, I Good
Peg - gy Sue.

wrapped the towel a - round me and I
gol - ly, Miss Mol - ly was a -

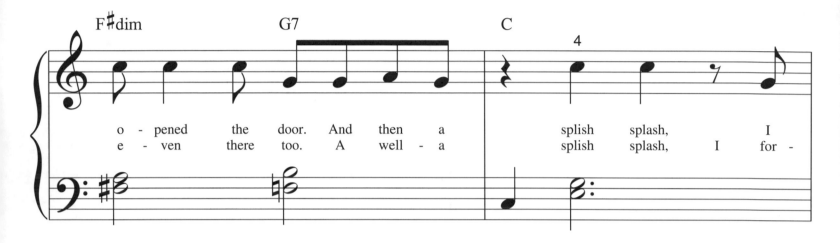

o - pened the door. And then a
e - ven there too. A well - a

splish splash, I
splish splash, I for -

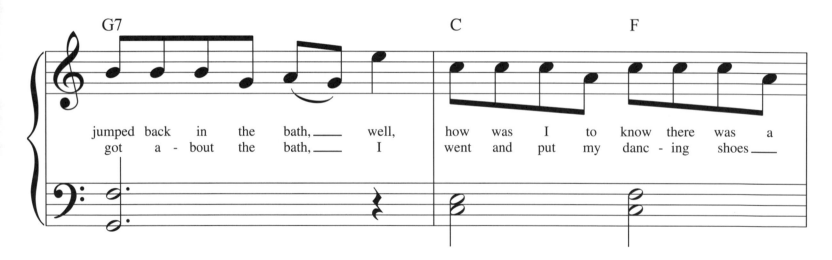

jumped back in the bath, ____ well,
got a - bout the bath, ____ I

how was I to know there was a
went and put my danc - ing shoes ____

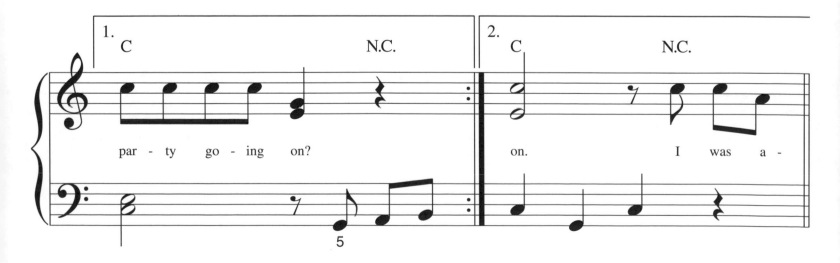

par - ty go - ing on?

on. I was a -

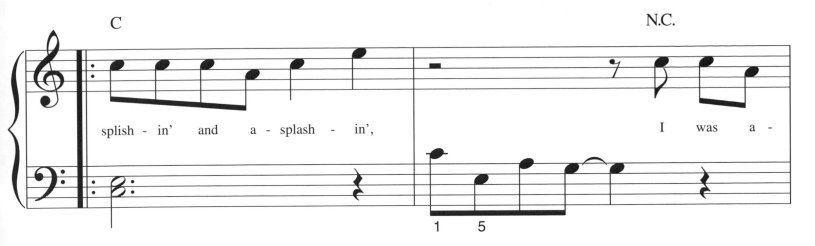

splish - in' and a - splash - in',   I was a -

roll - in' and a - stroll - in',   I was a

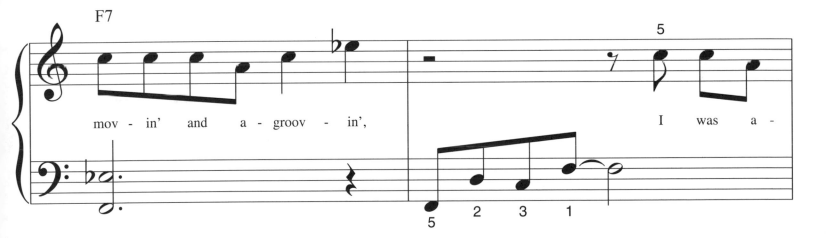

mov - in' and a - groov - in',   I was a -

Repeat and Fade

reel - in' with the feel - in',   I was a -

TWIST AND SHOUT

Words and Music by BERT RUSSELL
and PHIL MEDLEY

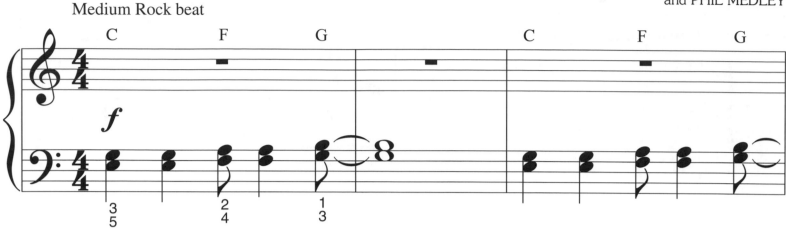

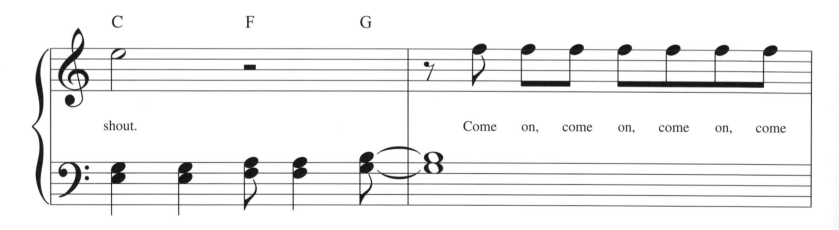

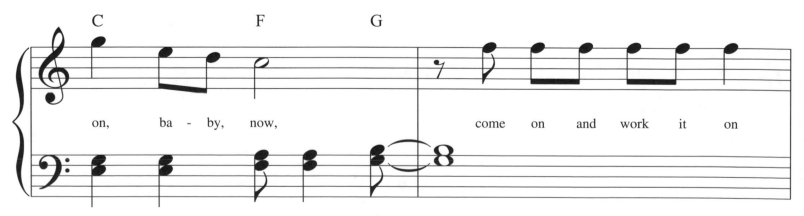

out.

Well,__ work it on out,_____
You know you twist, lit - tle girl,_____

you know you look   so   good,___   you know you got___ me___
you know you twist   so   fine,___   come on and twist a   lit - tle

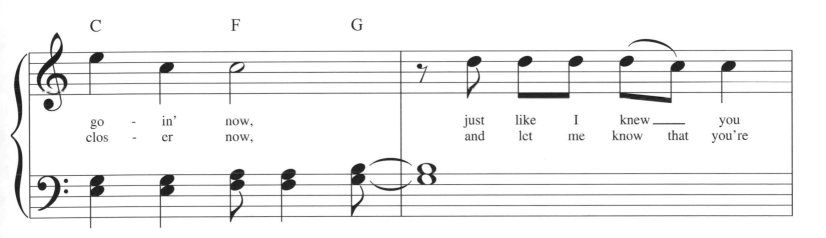

go - in' now,   just   like   I   knew_____   you
clos - er now,   and   let   me   know that   you're

D.C. and Fade

would.   Well, shake it up   Oo!
mine.

WOOLY BULLY

Words and Music by
DOMINGO SAMUDIO

Moderate Rock

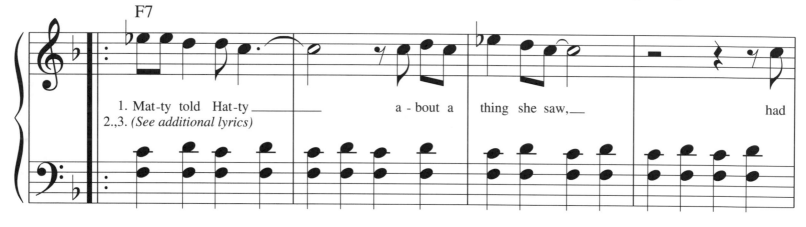

1. Mat-ty told Hat-ty _____ a-bout a thing she saw, _____ had
2.,3. *(See additional lyrics)*

two big horns _____ and a wool-y jaw. Wool-y Bul-ly _____

_____ Wool-y Bul-ly. _____ Wool-y

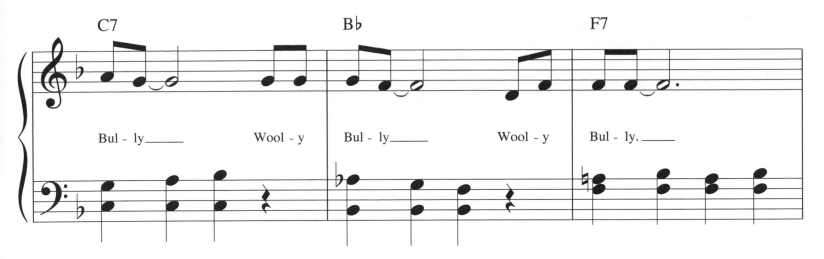

Additional Lyrics

2. Hatty told Matty
   Let's don't take no chance,
   Let's not be L7
   Come and learn to dance.
   Wooly bully wooly bully.
   Wooly bully wooly bully wooly bully.

3. Matty told Hatty
   That's the thing to do,
   Get yo' someone really
   To pull the wool with you.
   Wooly bully wooly bully.
   Wooly bully wooly bully wooly bully.

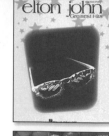

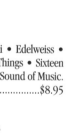